OLD TOKYO

OLD TOKYO

Walks in the City of the Shogun

SUMIKO ENBUTSU

illustrations by
Ryosuke Ishida

CHARLES E. TUTTLE COMPANY
Rutland, Vermont & Tokyo, Japan

Published by Charles E. Tuttle Company, Inc.
of Rutland, Vermont & Tokyo, Japan
with editorial offices at
2-6 Suido 1-chome, Bunkyo-ku, Tokyo 112

LCC Card No. 92-62458
ISBN 0-8048-1874-6

First edition, 1993

Printed in Japan

CONTENTS

ACKNOWLEDGMENTS

The original version of this book, *Discover Shitamachi,* was published in 1984 as the result of suggestions and assistance from my friends who regretted the lack of a useful walking guide to Tokyo. Many friends eagerly participated in testing my manuscript on the field, and some, in editing and proofreading the text. I am still indebted to those old friends whose cooperation was vital to the birth of the book. This book unfortunately went out of print in 1990.

In publishing this completely revised and updated version, I have once again relied upon the encouragement and support of many friends. I owe a special debt of gratitude to Mr. Ryosuke Ishida, a renowned paper-cut artist, whose atmospheric depictions of Shitamachi people and neighborhoods are used to introduce each area covered in the book. I also appreciate the permission of the ward offices of Chuo, Koto, Taito, Shinagawa, and Sumida wards to use some of the excellent photographs from their files. I also tender my heartfelt gratitude for the kind efforts of other individuals and organizations whose cooperation over the years has enabled the publication of this book. I express my deep gratitude and hope they will continue to be generous with their counsel and support in the future.

TOKYO OVERVIEW

Four hundred years ago, Tokyo was a vast stretch of wilderness. The sea reached deep inland, its water almost lapping at the base of the Imperial Palace. The Ginza and Tsukiji were under water, and Tokyo Station was in the middle of a marsh. To this desolate land came Tokugawa Ieyasu, a far-sighted samurai lord, who built a town there in 1590. He named it Edo, meaning "waterfront." Soon after Ieyasu's rise to the national leadership, this burgeoning town became the capital of Japan. He relaid the city plan and adopted an unprecedented spiral design originating from his castle. To secure political stability, he institutionalized various systems to promote national unity under a central feudal administration. Foreign contact was restricted, and peace prevailed in the country for nearly three centuries.

There was one thing which Ieyasu did not quite foresee, however. The new peace and stability sapped the samurai's energy, and the commoners who profited most from peace gained in eminence. Edo became a stage for merchants and craftsmen to display their economic and cultural vitality. Many Japanese things which are internationally appreciated, such as Kabuki, ukiyo-e, sushi, and tempura, to name but a few, are the products of these commoners' creativity. They lived in a densely populated area called Shitamachi, literally "the land below" (the castle). Adjacent to what is now the high-tech business hub of Tokyo, Shitamachi still harbors the energy and spirit of the old Edo commoners.

The original geography of the waterfront area discouraged all except the resourceful Ieyasu, who was soon to become the first of the Tokugawa shoguns. The setting was that of a frontier. In the east the Sumida River, large and untamed, discharged into the sea inundating the surrounding area with frequent floods. Patches of raised ground were dotted here and there, and some distance upstream stood Asakusa Kannon, an old temple dating from the seventh century. Down in the bay, the coast made a deep recess, forming an inlet called Hibiya. From there, the land rose in low hills rolling to the north and west. On the top of one of these hills was the abandoned residence of a medieval lord, the memory of his tragic assassination lurking in the ruins. A smaller stream, called the Hira River, flowed from here into the bay.

This uncultivated place was offered to Ieyasu in exchange for his original fief in Mikawa, which was closer to Kyoto and thus more civilized. Clearly, it was a scheme by wily Toyotomi Hideyoshi, the ruler at the time, who wanted to keep Ieyasu away from Kyoto, which had been the political center of Japan since the ninth century. Ieyasu accepted the offer in spite of his retainers' fierce objections. He saw a great future in the floodplain open to the sea. He also had confidence in the expertise of his civil-engineering staff. Thus, on August 1, 1590, he made his official entry into Edo and immediately set out to develop the lowland beneath the abandoned heights.

Ieyasu modeled his first city plan on Kyoto, which had been designed after Changan, the capital of Tang dynasty China. The ancient Chinese believed that a city plan had to satisfy certain geographic conditions based on the worship of the four gods of heaven. There should be a large river in the east for the Dragon God to live in. In the south there should be a lake or sea for the Phoenix to reside in. In the west a large road was to be guarded by the Tiger God; and in the north there should be a mountain where the God of Xuanwu, symbolized by a turtle entwined with snakes, could live. All told, the requirements provide for a sunny land sloping down to the sea, with a convenient water supply and easy routes to other areas.

To adapt this time-honored principle of city planning to Edo, Ieyasu had to turn the direction of his city plan about 100 degrees counterclockwise. This was an ingenious solution designed to dispel the worries of his vassals. Mt. Fuji, which is actually to the west of Edo, now came to the north, crowning the hilltop site of the abandoned mansion where Ieyasu was going to build his castle. The Hira River ran to the east of the castle; in the south spread Edo Bay; and in the west the Tokaido Highway, though not yet fully developed, led to Kamakura and Kyoto. It was also decided to protect the northeast direction of the city by building a major temple there, just as Kyoto had Enryaku-ji in its northeastern suburb. The northeast was considered an unlucky direction, vulnerable to invasion by evil spirits and enemies, needing a powerful magic to ward them off.

Hideyoshi died in the course of the project, in 1598. A crucial battle ensued between two camps of warring lords, one supporting Ieyasu, and the other siding with Hideyori, Hideyoshi's young heir. Ieyasu won a decisive victory and the national leadership as a result. As shogun, in 1603, he proclaimed Edo the new capital of Japan, replacing Kyoto. This decision required that the city be reorganized, and so Ieyasu canceled the plan to build a quasi-Kyoto and adopted a bold spiral design instead.

The uncoiling line of a spiral spreads indefinitely and therefore would facilitate the city's expansion. A spiraling waterway was built by connecting rivers, ponds, and already cut canals, starting at the castle and unfolding clockwise to reach the Sumida River. The water-filled channels served the dual purpose of providing easy access to the city center from the sea and blocking the advance of potential invaders. Edo Castle was magnificently redesigned to demonstrate the shogun's status. The highest tower ever built in Japan was constructed, surrounded by layers of massive stone walls; at its base, a complex maze of buildings was erected. It was an enormous project which required the work of three generations of shogun before its full completion in 1640. To implement the new city plan, it became necessary to fill the inlet of Hibiya. Part of a hill near Kanda was excavated to provide soil for the reclamation.

The resultant land became what is now Nihombashi, the Ginza, and Shimbashi.

A fabulous construction boom started all over Edo. The shogun's vassals competed in building splendid residences, lavishing money and energy on creating gorgeous buildings in highly ornate styles similar to those surviving in Nikko. Upon completion, they vied with each other in requesting the shogun to visit. If the shogun did indeed visit, a special gate and hall, also extravagantly constructed, were added to receive him and commemorate the visit. The most sensational construction was of course the castle itself. Guarded by circles of tall stone walls, a 63-meter-high, five-story tower soared on the 20-meter-high hill. The height of the tower and architectural complexity of the castle showed the high level of civil-engineering technology the Japanese had attained. Close to the castle, Nihombashi and its neighborhoods thronged with merchants who hurried from Osaka and Kyoto to capitalize on the new economic opportunities and workers gathered from nearby provinces to supply the much needed labor. Entertainers also came expecting generous audiences in the booming new city.

The first city of Edo was a real gem, although small by today's standards, including just Chiyoda-ku, Chuo-ku, and a slice of Minato-ku. The city was bounded to the east by the Sumida River, and no bridge was allowed to span the river for strategic reasons. It was, however, a many-splendored city as we see it depicted in silk screens and illustrations of the time. Nothing remains of it today, as a great conflagration reduced everything to ashes less than twenty years after its completion. On a windy day in January 1657, an ominous fire started at a temple, triggering a chain of blazes lasting for two days. The castle's fine tower was no exception to the disastrous destruction.

The shogunate moved fast to rebuild and even expand the city. More land was reclaimed from the sea, and the Sumida River was spanned by large bridges with a view to facilitating the city's eastward expansion. Financial assistance was given to both samurai and commoners to encourage speedy reconstruction. The first bridge built in 1660 was called Ryogokubashi, and soon the riversides began to thrive with visitors in all seasons. Tsukiji, to the south of Ginza, was reclaimed in order to move temples from the central city. The samurai residences were spread out, and major roads were broadened in an attempt to curb the spread of fire. However, the luxury and splendor of the initial Edo were never recovered, and the castle's tower was not rebuilt. By the end of the Edo period, the city had grown to cover eighteen of the twenty-three wards of present-day Tokyo, with an estimated population of one million and four hundred thousand—a figure based on the amount of rice consumed.

Space was alloted to residents of the city according to status. The area in front of the castle's front gate, including part of the reclaimed land, was given to the shogun's allies in the war of 1600, the neighboring area to the west was allotted to other lords who surrendered after the same war, and the area spreading to the east from behind the castle was given to the shogun's retainers and low-class samurai. Commoners were given Kanda and Nihombashi, which were close to both the castle and the sea. Roughly speaking, about 60 percent of the land was allotted to the warrior class, whose actual number was less than half the population. Commoners, who accounted for more than half the population, received only 20 percent of the land, and the remaining 20 percent went to temples and shrines, the inhabitants of which represented less than 5 percent.

Though given large estates in the city, the majority of samurai were not permanent residents. As a means of controlling more than two hundred lords, the shogun demanded that they spend each alternate year in Edo and leave their wives and heirs at their city residences as de facto hostages. The typical lord's Edo residence consisted of three separate locations: an upper house close to the castle, convenient for performing duties; a middle house for family residence; and a lower house which had a garden and warehouses for the storage of tools and commodities. Some of the famous gardens in Tokyo, such as

Rikugien or Korakuen, are the former lower houses of the foremost lords. The annual trip between Edo and the fief had to be made in a grand procession which matched the lord's status, the details of which were fastidiously specified by the shogunate. All this was intended to drain the resources of the lords and deprive them of the financial power to rebel.

The finances of the shogun's retainers, who were full-time residents of Edo, suffered particularly badly. To cover the cost of living in the city, they were compelled to sell the rice they received as stipends, and soon they found themselves at the mercy of rice dealers and loan sharks. They eked out a meager living from humble side jobs such as making umbrellas and growing potted plants. The smart ones shed their military status and contributed their skills in art and letters to the entertainment and publishing businesses.

In contrast to the sorry plight of the warrior class, the commoners were energetic and optimistic in spite of the rigid class system. Merchants capitalized on business opportunities, and craftsmen and workers on the bottom rung also enjoyed their life in Edo. Although they were herded into crowded housing and had no space to enjoy greenery, they placed potted plants outside front doors and along the narrow alleys between tenements—a scene still visible in Shitamachi today. The money obtained even after hard work was minimal, and every member of the family had to work. However, to those who did not aspire to accumulate material wealth, life in Edo could be fun, with neither tax on residents in tenements nor fear of unemployment. When artists and writers praised the prosperity of Edo, their descriptions were always of brisk business, crowded theaters, and quarters of light and merriment in the commoners' districts. One example is Hiroshige's serialized woodblock prints entitled, *One Hundred Famous Spots in Edo*. This was the last of his highly celebrated landscape series, rendered in three years from 1856 to 1859. The artist died in September of the same year as its completion. The focus of his attention was the vibrant Shitamachi towns.

The art of printing from woodblocks came from Kyoto, where there had been a long history of printing sutras and scholastic books. A little before the Edo period, this technique was applied to the printing of practical information and children's picture books. Kyoto publishers expanded to Edo to cater to the huge warrior population in the city. They produced a best seller: a samurai directory listing the names, positions, family crests, and other information about each lord and his retainers. Edo commoners borrowed this idea to publish a Kabuki actors' directory and a Yoshiwara (red-light district) guide in exactly the same style. Genre paintings were also developed in Kyoto and Osaka, where portraits of fashionable women were painted on silk and treasured by wealthy merchants. Ukiyo-e popularized these art forms by mass production, printing from woodblocks onto paper.

Kabuki, particularly the dynamic style called Edo Kabuki, reflected the commoners' taste for lively and colorful stages. The development of Kabuki in Kyoto and Osaka centered on episodes which took place in red-light districts and presented detailed love scenes. The style thus created is called *wagoto* and is rather feminine in nature. By contrast, the people of Edo preferred to see acts of rough bravado which seemed to match more closely the brisk atmosphere of the newly constructed city. Ichikawa Danjuro and Danjuro II created the art of highly exaggerated makeup and vigorous acting. This bravado style was called *aragoto* and was effective in presenting young heroes who were motivated by righteous indignation. After the mid-eighteenth century, Edo Kabuki emerged from the influence of Kyoto and Osaka and established its own preeminence in presenting plays of dramatic vitality.

The term *Edokko* (child of Edo) was established in the mid-eighteenth century when genuine natives of Edo emerged at the forefront of economic and cultural life for the first time. The first generations of merchants who had branched out from western Japan were tightly controlled by their headquarters and had not localized for a long time. Typical businesses originated in Edo were the fish market at Nihombashi and rice and monetary transactions at Kuramae. The merchants in these trades rapidly amassed fortunes and spent generously on Kabuki, parties at the Yoshiwara, and festivals. Craftsmen and workers participated in the growth of broad-based popular culture.

When the Tokugawa regime eventually collapsed, and the Meiji Restoration brought about the birth of modern Japan in 1868, the samurai fled back to their provinces in a state of panic. Their beautiful Edo residences were abandoned and left to ruin. The new mayor of Tokyo (Eastern Capital), as Edo was renamed, ordered in 1869 that the former samurai districts should be turned into farms to grow tea and mulberry bushes. Much later, the large sites of feudal lords were redeveloped into office buildings, universities, and residential quarters. In the rush to westernize, rows of brick buildings were built in the Ginza, a lackluster commercial district in the Edo period, but the project ended in a disastrous failure owing to poor construction. Many plans were proposed for the transformation of the feudal city into a new city matching its new name. However, no overhaul of the city was made for reasons of conflicting interests among political and business leaders, and lack of money. Therefore, the spiral of Ieyasu can still be discerned today.

In the twentieth century, Tokyo was flattened twice—by the Great Kanto Earthquake in 1923 and by heavy air raids during World War II. Each time, the citizens were quick to clear the debris and build anew. Now, as a key world financial and business center, Tokyo competes in efficiency and comfort with New York and London. Soaring hotels and office buildings equipped with some of the most advanced high-tech facilities have mushroomed in the central districts in the 1980s. Traffic congestion is almost perennial. Many people argue against the city's continuing expansion and propose the decentralization of some of its functions. Not immune to these changes, Shitamachi faces an important challenge now. How to protect its traditional lifestyles and values from avid developers has been a crucial concern in the past several years, and citizens have often displayed their vitality and wisdom in saving landmarks. Despite recent redevelopment, Shitamachi still abounds in opportunities to come in close contact with old Tokyo and a mix of interesting people.

This guidebook will help English-speaking residents and visitors to Tokyo enjoy the flavor of the premodern city. Simple directions to each Shitamachi town are given, and all are accessible by Tokyo's public transportation system, which is one of the best in the world. If one complete course proves too time consuming, it is always possible to shorten the tour by using midway train stations indicated in the guide. Any map of Tokyo's train and subway network will be a good companion to this book. *The Tokyo Transit Book* by Garry Bassin is useful because it shows individual lines and transfers in designated colors and has the station names in both Japanese and romanized letters. It might be good to learn the following questions to ask while showing the Japanese names of your next destination:

Doko desu ka? (Where is this?)
Gozonji desu ka? (Do you know this?)

Inquiries made to the listed telephone numbers should be in Japanese only. The walking times given do not include time for sightseeing, eating, or shopping, so allow a couple of hours depending on your schedule and interests.

For your convenience in ordering at restaurants, various dishes have been recommended. Most of the eating places in the book are modest establishments catering to local people, and prices are reasonable. It might be wise to try to avoid the lunch time rush which for most workers in Japan is between 12:00 and 1:00 P.M., particularly when the restaurant of your choice is located in a business district.

ASAKUSA

Walking time
Kannon temple area: 1 hour
North Asakusa: 1–2 hours
Kappabashi: 45 minutes

BACKGROUND For more than fourteen centuries Asakusa has captured people's hearts; it is loved for its temple, history, fun shopping, and easy accessibility. The Asakusa Kannon temple, or Senso-ji, is of course the main attraction. The temple is dedicated to Kannon, a Buddhist bodhisattva revered for her compassion for human weakness and suffering; because of the simplicity of the teachings involved in worshiping her, Kannon has been popular throughout the country since early times. Of the numerous temples dedicated to Kannon, Asakusa Kannon is one of the best known.

The streams of people who daily flood the area, however, seem less interested in Kannon than in the colorful shopping streets. The temple itself is not grandiose and lacks the majestic dignity normally associated with such venerable religious establishments. What is really impressive about the area are the bustling businesses which cater to the visitors' secular needs and whose profusion almost obscures the temple's presence.

This area once formed the core of a vigorous common people's culture which blossomed brilliantly from the mid-eighteenth century until the early twentieth century. Both the Yoshiwara red-light district and many Kabuki theaters used to be located near here, and the area's booming entertainment business survived into the 1960s. Many lament Asakusa's lost

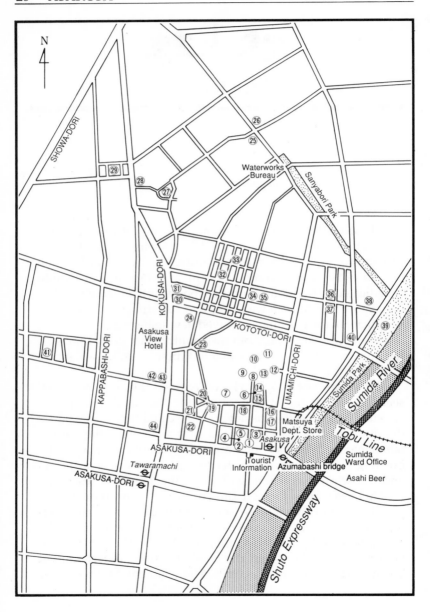

glory, but what is left is more than sufficient for you to feel its vitality and to sense the shadowy presence of old traditions. This is particularly true if you extend your walk into the backstreets, both inside and outside the temple compound.

GETTING THERE   To get to Asakusa, take the Ginza Line to Asakusa Station, the line's terminal. Get off the train and take the stairway in the middle of the platform. After passing through the ticket gate, turn right and take Exit 1 to come out on the street. Walk straight past several shops until you see the front gate of the Asakusa Kannon temple with its huge lantern. Across the street to your left is the Tourist Information Center.

ASAKUSA KANNON TEMPLE (Senso-ji 浅草寺**)**   The front gate, often depicted in old woodblock prints and contemporary photographs, is called **Kaminarimon** 雷門 ①, or the gate *(mon)* of the god of thunder (Kaminari). His statue is housed in the left-hand section of the gate and a statue of the god of wind is in the right-hand section. The gate itself is a postwar reproduction of its predecessor which was destroyed by fire in 1865. Neighbors managed to save the heads of the two gods from the flames, and a little later, the bodies were reproduced. More recently, in 1978, another pair of statues was donated in commemoration of the 1,350th anniversary of Kannon's first appearance at Asakusa. These are the dragon gods carved by Denchu Hiragushi, enshrined in the rear sections of the gate.

Just to the left of the gate, on the main street, **Tokiwado** 常盤堂 ② is a busy shop which sells traditional sweets called *okoshi*. *Okoshi* are a little like popcorn balls, but made from different ingredients, and have always been one of the most popular souvenirs of Asakusa. A demonstration stall is set up to show how they are made and a jar containing free samples is placed nearby. On the other side of the gate, in a black-and-white building with several wooden shop signs on the facade, is an interesting paper-crafts shop called **Kurodaya** 黒田屋 ③; it is nice to browse among shelves of colorful *chiyogami* (printed

Japanese paper), paper crafts, and unusual stationery items.

Passing through the gate, you will find a colorfully decorated shopping lane called Nakamise, which leads straight to
the main hall of the temple. On weekends and holidays, the
street is so crowded that you just have to give yourself up to the
flow of people. There are nearly one hundred shops in this area
alone, each teeming with toys, food, women's accessories, and
clothes. Hundreds more line the side streets, which branch off
in both directions.

These shops have evolved from the Edo-period souvenir
vendors who set up stalls on the borders of subsidiary temples
around here. After the Meiji Restoration, the government reorganized the whole compound and put the shops in apartment-
like buildings as you see now. Though most of the shops have
changed hands since then, several continue to be operated by
the same families. For instance, **Kaneso** かね惣 ④ has special-
ized in traditional cutlery since the Edo period. Turn left at the
end of the first small block of shops and look for a shop on your
left. Opposite this shop is **Bunsendo** 文扇堂 ⑤, which sells
pretty Japanese fans with designs of imaginary creatures such
as the *kappa* (river imp), or the fat-faced lady called *otafuku*.
Back at the main thoroughfare, you might notice an appetizing
smell. It comes from a shop called **Iidaya** 飯田屋 about halfway
down toward the main hall. The smell is that of soy sauce used
for broiling *sembei* (rice crackers) on a charcoal grill. As you
watch a man busily turning flat, round pieces of rice dough,
you might be tempted to buy one to nibble along the way. The
most fascinating shop of all—in fact the only one of its kind in
Tokyo—is **Sukeroku** 助六 ⑥, located almost at the end of
Nakamise on the right. The display shelves of the 2-yard-wide
shop are filled with ingeniously crafted miniature toys, handmade by traditional craftsmen. Kimura-san, the shop's owner,
is happy to receive foreign visitors and explain the techniques
and workmanship involved.

The fenced area in front of Sukeroku is the **Dembo-in** 伝法
院 ⑦, the chief abbot's residence, known for its beautiful gar-

den. The large red gate to its right is the **Hozomon** 宝蔵門 ⑧ (Treasure Storage Gate), so called because its upper section is used as a repository for rare sutras and other temple valuables. A pair of guardian gods, called Nio, are enshrined in the side sections, and so the gate is also called the Niomon which is a more familiar name. Nio, always in a pair, are guardians who are supposed to frighten evil spirits away from the principal deity enshrined in the main hall.

At the rear of the gate are hung huge *waraji* (straw sandals) donated by farmers from northern Japan. Supposed to be worn by the Nio, they are much too large even for the 5.5-meter gods, whose feet seem to be, at best, about 1 meter. Given the legendary size of the Kannon enshrined here, which is about 6 centimeters, the scale of the sizes between the sandals, the guardian statues, and the Kannon statue itself, is quite amusing.

To your left is a **red-and-gold pagoda** 五重塔 ⑨, which was rebuilt in 1970. Its predecessor was donated by the third Tokugawa shogun, Iemitsu, and erected on the other side of the Hozomon gate. The current tower is a ferroconcrete structure in the same design, retaining the features of the complex woodwork of the seventeenth-century original. On the top story, particles of Lord Buddha's bones, acquired as a gift from a Sri Lankan temple, are kept in a golden container hung from the ceiling. The pagoda is open to the public three times a year on February 15, April 8, and December 8, the dates related to Lord Buddha's death, birth, and enlightenment respectively.

When you wish to get permission to view the old garden of Dembo-in, which is described later, you should go to an office here. Enter the door in the left-hand section of the tower base and walk up the stairs to the right. At the third door on your left, ask the clerk for permission to see the garden. After signing your name and address in a notebook, you will be given a free ticket for entry into the garden, unless it is reserved for a special occasion.

In front of the **main hall** 本堂 ⑩, clouds of heavily-scented purple smoke rise continuously from a large bronze incense burner. People are seen wafting the smoke to different parts of their bodies, as it is believed that the parts exposed to the smoke will be cured of ailments.

Inside the main hall, people of all ages throw coins into an offering box and pray briefly. Kannon is supposed to be enshrined in the glittering gold inner shrine seen through the net screen. All the monks of the temple gather at the altar to chant sutras three times a day. The daily services, constant stream of worshipers, flickering candles, painted ceiling, and even the air in the building speak eloquently of its long history as a special place for the prayers of high and low alike.

The origin of Senso-ji is a mystery. According to a legend, two brothers caught a 2-inch golden statue in their nets in the year 628, while fishing in the nearby Sumida River. Awe-struck by the dignity of the little figure, they took it to their village head, who immediately recognized it as a statue of the merciful Kannon and had it enshrined in his thatched house. The Kannon was worshiped by all the villagers, and word spread about the rare statue, which attracted many people. The village and temple grew; services and crafts catering to the temple and its visitors thrived. Strangely enough, there is no known witness or firm evidence to prove the actual existence of the small statue.

The Tokugawa shoguns paid special respect to this temple and donated land and splendid buildings. The wealth and popularity of the temple were sufficient to support numerous subsidiary temples and shrines which filled the extensive compound, forming a kind of religious kingdom. The chaotic variety of gods and the various wonders they were supposed to achieve has increased the temple's fame and popularity.

ASAKUSA-JINJA 浅草神社 Another large building to the left of the temple is the shrine, **Asakusa-jinja** ⑪, dedicated to the two fishermen and their village head, hence its alias, Sanja, which means "three shrines." Donated by Shogun Iemitsu in 1649, this shrine is designated an important cultural asset. You may take a closer look at the interior decorations of the building from the top landing of the stairway. (Take your shoes off, please.) The compound, which is usually quiet, overflows with people in the middle of May, when the Sanja Matsuri festival commemorates the discoverers of the Kannon. More than a hundred *omikoshi* (portable shrines) and their bearers, representing different areas in the shrine's parish, bustle in the space to the left of the shrine. The three *omikoshi* of the shrine, representing the three founders of the temple, solemnly march out from the compound onto the street to lead the daylong festival parade. As one of the three most exciting festivals in Tokyo, the spectacular event thrills the hearts of festival buffs. Another *omikoshi* parade is held in October, and in November an historic pageant celebrates Ieyasu's entry into Edo over four-hundred years ago.

As you leave the shrine through its torii, on the left is **Nitemmon** 二天門 ⑫, which also dates from the mid-seventeenth century. These two buildings escaped the air raids during World War II, but the main building, pagoda, and the two front gates were lost and have subsequently been rebuilt with concrete. The slips of paper pasted on the pillars and walls of this gate are called *senja-fuda*, which means literally "one thousand shrine card." These are name cards left by worshipers as proof of their visits. They use a special calligraphy called *Edo moji* (Edo letters), preferred because of its powerful, decorative strokes. The cards are custom-printed, and the more decorative ones are collected as a hobby.

As you walk straight away from Asakusa-jinja toward the front gate, there are two **bronze buddhas** 二尊仏 ⑬, which although beautiful are seldom noticed. They are gracefully executed despite their large size, and look particularly beautiful when the surrounding gingko trees take on autumn colors. The statues were donated in 1687 by a rice dealer, Takase Zenbee, to pray for the repose of the soul of his dead master, who was a wealthy rice dealer. Takase himself was the manager of the rice store, but the once prosperous store went bankrupt due to the squandering of the master and his son. After becoming independent, Takase nonetheless felt obligated to express his appreciation to his former employer in this manner.

Behind the buddhas is a small mound with a belfry next to a red shrine dedicated to Benten. Archaeologists have concluded that the hill is an ancient burial mound from articles suggesting prehistoric human habitation which were excavated here. This bell was one of the public time-bells used to toll the hours of the day during the Edo period. It is now rung daily at 6:00 A.M., at which time the front gate of the temple is opened to let ardent worshipers in. The bell is also rung on New Year's Eve.

TRADITIONAL SHOPS   Turn right and walk straight on. The first shop on the corner, **Nakaya** 中屋 ⑭ , carries casual wear and small interior furnishings. A charming house next to it is **Kure Mutsu** 暮六つ, a saké drinking place. Its name means "the evening six" and is a carry-over from the Edo period when the 6:00 P.M. tolling of the time-bell indicated the time to stop work for the day. The third shop is a unique cosmetics shop, **Hyakusuke** 百助, which enjoys the patronage of Kabuki actors, traditional dancers, and geisha. Beautiful cosmetic brushes of different shapes and sizes are displayed in the window. An unobtrusive pink paper package decorated with white plum blossoms contains the makings for an old-time beauty pack, a powder of nightingales' droppings. This was used quite extensively in prewar years for beautifying the face.

Three houses away from this shop, **Fujiya** ふじや ⑮ specializes in traditional cotton cloth dyed with various designs. *(Open 10:00-22:00. Closed on Thursdays.)* You can recognize the shop by its blue and white *noren* with a wisteria *(fuji)* flower design. All the products sold here are of one size, but the rich variety is overwhelming. The cotton cloth is called *tenugui*, which literally means "hand cleaning cloth," but is more like a large kerchief and was widely used among people of the Edo period. Even today, festival participants and working-class people wind them attractively around their heads, and Kabuki actors use them on stage or as gifts with their names or favorite designs dyed on. One *tenugui* sold at the shop shows various ways of wearing it on the head according to one's sex, social standing, or occasion. In the early history of *tenugui* longer ones were used for sashes, but the length became standardized to about 3 feet during the Edo period. The width is always 1 foot, the size of traditional looms. The postwar advent of towels and tissue paper caused the rapid decline of *tenugui* in everyday use, but Kawakami-san of Fujiya strove hard to call attention to their artistry. His success is evident in the shop's prosperity.

Leaving Fujiya, turn right to come to a crossroads. Your basic direction is to the right but there are a few good, small restaurants along the street just ahead. On the left corner is a sweet shop selling fried dumplings. Next to it is **Kintaro** 金太楼 ⑯, a sushi bar which offers special prices on *nigiri* and *chirashi* at lunch time. *(Open 11:30-23:00. Usually closed on Tuesdays.)* In the next small block, also on the left, is **Keyaki** 欅 ⑰, a small, cozy restaurant whose entrance is marked by a white paper lantern and a rope curtain at the doorway. Choose one of the set menus of tempura or sashimi with rice and soup. *(Open 11:00-14:00, 17:00-20:00. Closed on Mondays.)* Further down, at **Towada** 十和田, a man can often be seen demonstrating the preparation of buckwheat noodles.

Turning right after Fujiya, however, you will see some more specialty shops, selling such things as gorgeous kimono for Japanese dancing, abacuses, turtle-shell crafts, and combs. **Yonoya** よのや ⑱ exhibits elaborately crafted traditional combs made of boxwood. The prices seem high, but the wonderfully smooth touch of the handmade combs keeps luring customers. At the next corner on the left, people are often seen standing in a long line in front of a tempura restaurant which has been much publicized in magazines and on television. Past it, you will see a big black wooden gate on your right. This is the side entrance to the Dembo-in garden 伝法院庭園.

DEMBO-IN GARDEN   Enter through a small door in the gate and walk through another wooden door across the courtyard straight ahead of you. Hand in your ticket (see page 23) at the house at the end of the alley. (Call if there is nobody around.) Passing under a connecting corridor on your left, you will come out to a big garden with a deep pond in the center. The construction of this garden is often attributed to Kobori Enshu, a celebrated garden designer and tea-ceremony master of the early seventeenth century, but some people argue that it is much older.

On the right is a big wooden house of simple beauty with another house on the left. In front of the second house sits a rectangular hollow stone, supposedly a stone coffin used for the burial of an ancient inhabitant. The temple bell placed by the pond was cast in 1387 and is the oldest in Tokyo.

Make your way to the right and meander down the path. You will enjoy the changing landscape as you walk. Except for the distant view of highrises surrounding the garden, the quiet atmosphere makes you forget that you have just come from the noisy, cluttered Nakamise. A small tea-ceremony house is nestled in the woods. The elegant building was originally made in the 1780s in Nagoya, copied from a tea house in Kyoto designed by Sen-no Rikyu, the famous tea-ceremony master. The original in Kyoto was lost in a fire. Continuing along the path which bends to the left, you will come out to a sunny shore.

Retrace your steps to the black gate on the street and turning right, you will come to a five-street intersection. If you would like a coffee break, **Royal** ローヤル珈琲店 ⑲ is recommended. Turn left and look for a dark brown building on the left. *(Open 9:00-21:00. Closed on the first, third, and fourth Tuesdays, and second Thursday and Friday of the month.)*

To continue, you should walk along the nearby colored walkway. **Tentake** 天健 ⑳, the first shop on this street, is another cozy tempura restaurant known among local people. Their specialty is a large ball-shaped *kakiage* (a fritter of small shrimps), but regular *tendon* and tempura are also good. *(Closed on Mondays.)*

ENTERTAINMENT DISTRICT   You will soon come to a relatively large street lined with many movie theaters. This area is called **Rokku,** or "Block Six," and used to be a bustling entertainment center. After the Meiji Restoration, the government divided up the temple compound into several blocks and designated the sixth block for street entertainers and performing-arts theaters which had previously been scattered around the main hall. With fewer banners and front-of-house advertisements, and with chic modern shops making inroads, it is difficult to imagine the vigor and pride the area had in the old days. A theater on the other side of the crossing, with banners in front and a couple of touts calling in guests, presents the traditional performing art of *rakugo* in which the actor assumes various characters while remaining seated on a cushion on the stage. The classical stories have been polished over a period of two hundred years, and the audience usually knows most of them, yet the stories remain extremely attractive and amusing when told by seasoned actors. Developed during the Edo period, this narrative art was particularly popular among the commoners who could not afford to go to expensive Kabuki theaters.

Rokku was the place where Japan's top entertainment thrived in prewar and early postwar years. Japanese performing artists eagerly learned the hottest Western music, vaudevilles, and operettas, and adapted them for the domestic audience. Japan's first movie theater for permanent shows was built here in 1903, followed by many more afterwards.

Your basic direction is to the right along the main road of Rokku. However, a short detour to the left will take you to a *sembei* shop, **Hinode** 日乃出せんべい ㉑, a little off the main road to the left. Further beyond is another *sembei* shop, **Iriyama** 入山, where customers are often waiting for the next round of broiling. Next to Iriyama is **Towada** 十和田 ㉒, which serves good noodles, as well as *kaiseki* dinner upon reservation. *(Open 11:00-22:00 throughout the year. Tel: 3841-7375.)*

Retrace your steps and continue straight until the end of the main road of Rokku, where you should bear right. At this point you will see a high tower with swinging chairs, which is part of a playground called **Hanayashiki** 花屋敷 ㉓. If you wish to finish your tour here, you can turn right and go back to the main hall, where you should walk down the shopping lane and out the front gate. Otherwise, enter the roofed arcade on your left and walk straight on. Past a large sukiyaki restaurant with red-and-white lanterns hung across its entrance, you will find **Adachiya** あだちや ㉔ on the left, specializing in authentic festival outfits. Things such as *happi* coats, pants, *tabi* (divided-toe socks) and *waraji* are sold here. In the left-hand section of the shop are shelves piled with traditional cotton work shirts of various textile designs. Next to Adachiya, a public facility exhibiting traditional handicrafts is open throughout the year. On two weekends a month, craftsmen take turns in demonstrating their skills. *(Open 10:00-21:00. Tel: 3847-2587.)* Small paper lanterns are sold at a lantern shop across the street. The two kanji characters for Asakusa are already written on them, and other names can be added upon purchase. These might make a special souvenir from your trip. The street soon meets with a larger street, where you can turn left and left again at the next traffic light to reach Tawaramachi Station in about ten minutes. Time and energy permitting, continue to explore the northern part of Asakusa.

NORTH ASAKUSA

At the end of the roofed arcade, cross the main street and walk straight on. This street, called Senzoku-dori, used to be a short-cut through the rice paddies to the Yoshiwara district. The route is now lined with numerous shops, but is still traceable to the former pleasure district.

*   *   *

SUGGESTED DETOUR: Keep walking straight for about ten minutes until you come to a crossing with a major street. The Waterworks Bureau, a large, drab, concrete building, stands on the left. Turn left and walk to the second traffic light. Just before the signal, a lanky willow tree is a reminder of the famous **"Look-back Willow"** 見返り柳 ㉕ of the Edo period, so called because overnight visitors to the Yoshiwara turned around here to look back at their special women when they left in the morning. The gate of the Yoshiwara was at this crossroads, and the gently curving street to the left retains the Yoshiwara's original street plan.

Before entering the curving street, you might be interested in two traditional restaurants on the other side of the main street. **Iseya** 伊勢屋 ㉖, at the first small street beyond the intersection, serves good tempura. The dark, glossy wood inside suggests the shop's long history. For lunch, *tendon* is recommended. *(Open 11:30-14:30, 17:00-20:00. Closed on Wednesdays.)* Next to Iseya is **Nakae** 中江, a horsemeat restaurant operating since the Edo period. Horsemeat was called *ketobashi*, which means "kick away" and was popular among visitors to the Yoshiwara who thought the meat was effective in keeping away venereal diseases. The meat is lean and is served as sashimi or cooked at your table like sukiyaki. *(Open 15:00-22:00 on weekdays, 12:00-22:00 on Sundays and holidays. Closed on Mondays.)* Straight ahead along the main street is Minowa Station on the Hibiya Line.

Although nothing remains of it now, the Yoshiwara continued to operate until 1958. Walking down the main thoroughfare and bearing left at its end, you will come to a shrine, **Yoshiwara Benten** 吉原弁天 ㉗, on the left. The 2.5-meter-high bronze statue of Benten is dedicated to the unfortunate women of the Yoshiwara who died during the Great Kanto Earthquake of 1923. Every year on September 1, an anniversary service is held for them.

Cross the street, turn left, and take the first right. Walk down the curving road to the next major street crossing where if you turn right you will find **Otori-jinja** 鷲神社 ㉘, famous for its lucky-rake fairs held in November, when rows of makeshift stalls fill the compound, overflowing with gaudily colored bamboo rakes symbolizing good luck and fertility. Cross at the traffic lights and take the first right and you will find **Bon** 梵 ㉙, a restaurant which serves excellent Zen cuisine. *(Open 12:00– 18:00. Closed on Tuesdays. Tel: 3872-0375.)*

To go home, however, turn left and walk for about fifteen minutes to Tawaramachi subway station on the Ginza Line. Stay on the left side of the street until you see the towering highrise of Asakusa View Hotel on the other side of the street. Cross the street toward it and turn left to reach the subway station.

*   *   *

If you are not interested in the site of the Yoshiwara, turn left at the first crossing on Senzoku-dori. On the left of the street is a wonderful drinking place, **Ichimon** 一文 ㉚, marked by a willow tree in a corner and a big wooden tub above the gate. This is an ideal place to relax with your friends. When you enter through the sliding door, you buy the shop's currency, wooden tablets in denominations of 10, 5, and 1 *mon*. The *mon* was the lowest unit of currency used among the Edo-period commoners, hence the shop's name, Ichimon. At this shop, 1 mon represents ¥100, and if you buy about 50 *mon* per head to start with, it will usually be enough for a couple of bottles of saké, a tray of hors d'oeuvres, plus a dish or two. You can buy more money later, and the surplus will be refunded when you leave. Try some of their tofu dishes, such as *agedashi* (fried tofu in light sauce), *ichimon* steak, or the day's sashimi. *(Open 17:00–23:00. Closed on Sundays and holidays.)*

Turning right at the main street beyond Ichimon, you will come to **Funakin** 鮒金 ㉛ which sells *tsukudani* (fish and seaweed boiled down in soy sauce). An attractive lantern hung in front lends charm to the traditional appearance of the shop. Their speciality, *suzumeyaki* (skewered river fish), has a delicate flavor worth a try. Past Funakin, take the first right to return to Senzoku-dori which is five small blocks further down. Turn left and at the next traffic light, cross the street and turn right. Soon, a distinctly traditional building is seen on the left, with a tiled roof and facade resembling that of a shrine or temple. This is a public bath called **Akebonoyu** 曙湯 ㉜. Its stately roofs and plastered walls are very typical of Tokyo-style public bath architecture. Your direction is straight on, but near here is an excellent *soba* restaurant, **Daikokuya** 大黒屋 ㉝. Turn left at the corner of Akebonoyu and take the third right. Daikokuya is relatively new, but has established a reputation among connoisseurs of *soba* as one of the best places in Tokyo. Try the savory *seiro* (plain noodles) with or without tempura. In winter, *kamo suki* (duck and vegetables cooked on the table) is a real treat. There is also a good selection of *jizake* (provincial saké). Buckwheat noodles were a great favorite of the Edo commoners. Today, Sugano-san, the cook and owner, faces a great challenge in preserving the traditional flavor of this simple food, now that agricultural and environmental changes have altered the taste of many ingredients. *(Open 12:00–15:00, 17:00–23:00. Closed on Tuesdays. Tel: 3874-2986.)* Continuing straight from Akebonoyu, turn right at the next traffic light. In the second block on the left, a large building with a bold lattice design on the second level is **Kenban** 見番 ㉞, where reservations for geisha are made.

Turn left at the corner of Kenban. A big compound with gray walls on the right is a *machiai,* a house available upon reservation for an evening party complete with dinner and geisha entertainment. It stands on the site of a Kabuki theater which prospered in the Meiji era. Another large house next to it is also a *machiai.* Rows of big black cars with chauffeurs are often parked around here in the evening. Across the street from the second *machiai* is the annex of **Ichimon** 一文別館 ㉟, which comes alive with candle-lit lanterns in the evening. Continue straight on and turn left at the second crossing with a futon shop on the left. Turn right at the first traffic light. This area is part of a large footwear and leather-product center which extends from the east side of the Kannon temple.

Cross the street at the next traffic light and walk straight on. Soon a greenish-gray, tile-covered, five-story building appears on the right. It is a shoe wholesaler called **Suganuma** スガヌマ, with the company signboard projecting from the wall. At the farthest corner of the building, turn left for a quick look at a stone monument which shows the site of an Edo-period Kabuki theater, **Moritaza** 守田座 ㊱, erected at the entrance to a garage of the second building on the left. Retrace your steps to the Suganuma building and keep straight to find the site of yet another Kabuki theater, **Ichimuraza** 市村座 ㊲, by an electricity pole. This area, called Saruwaka-machi, used to host many theaters that were moved here as part of the shogunate's administrative reform. In Hiroshige's *A Night Scene at Saruwaka-machi*, a street extends straight from the foreground to the center of the picture; a full moon hangs in the hazy sky; and enraptured audiences have just come out onto the street after the close of the curtain. The theater district here was rather short-lived, however, due to the collapse of the Tokugawa shogunate.

Back at the crossroads with the Suganuma building on the corner, turn right and walk straight on. Cross the next intersection toward a temple, **Matsuchiyama Shoden** 待乳山聖天 ㊳, on elevated ground on the left. As you walk up the stone stairway, notice the temple symbols: money bags and forked daikon on both sides of the steps. Matsuchiyama Shoden, founded in the early seventeenth century, is dedicated to a pair of esoteric gods in ecstatic embrace; the posture is said to represent conjugal harmony. Daikon were regarded as having an invigorating effect when eaten, and two-pronged daikon, resembling legs, especially symbolized sex. Sexual fertility was associated with both business prosperity and wealth, and this temple attracts a steady stream of worshipers. On January 7, the temple holds a daikon festival. Worshipers bring daikon as offerings to the gods and are treated to cooked daikon—as magical food—to bring good luck in the coming year.

The temple stands on a very old hill. According to an ancient legend, thirty years before the Kannon's appearance in the Sumida River, there was a great famine and drought. When people prayed for the mercy of the gods, the ground rose in the area of Matsuchiyama. A golden dragon came down from heaven and coiled itself around the newly created hill. There followed a pouring rain which saved the people and their crops. Senso-ji's annual festival on March 18 is based on this story and features a golden dragon parade.

The hill used to command an excellent view of the Sumida River lined with hundreds of cherry trees. A canal branching off the Sumida ran behind the hill, leading to the Yoshiwara. A highly fashionable pastime in the Edo period was to hire a boat from Yanagibashi for a visit to the Yoshiwara, sailing upstream the Sumida River and turning left here. The canal, boat trips, and nightless pleasure district in the distance inspired Hiroshige and many other artists in their numerous prints and paintings. As you return to the stairway, look at the wall on the left. It is made of old roof tiles and is one of the few Edo-period landmarks remaining. At the bottom of the steps turn left to come to a T-junction, beyond which you will find **Sumida Park** 隅田公園 ㊴.

To return to Asakusa Station, you can go through the park, walking along the gently curving lane lined with cherry trees. You will walk under overpasses for cars and trains until finally you come out to the Azumabashi bridge with the spectacular buildings of Asahi Breweries and Sumida Ward Office on the other side of the river. The subway entrance is at a large intersection to the right. You may also walk along the busy main street. Near the first major intersection is **Miyamoto Unosuke Shoten** 宮本卯之助商店 ㊵, a maker of percussion and festival instruments. Back at the intersection, cross the Kototoi-dori road, and keep walking straight on. Past a railway overpass extending from the second level of a building, you will see a subway entrance sign on the right leading to the basement of Matsuya Department Store.

KAPPABASHI

Kappabashi, another extremely interesting neighborhood, spe-cializes in supplies for catering services and restaurants. Nu-merous shops are crammed together, selling all kinds of equipment and utensils for professional kitchens. If you wish to visit this area as an extension of your Asakusa Kannon tour, the easiest way would be to go back to Kaminarimon, turn right and walk straight until you come to a large T-junction. Cross the street, turn left, and walk to the next major intersec-tion. On this corner is the exit of Tawaramachi Station on the Ginza Line, where you get off if coming from central Tokyo. Turn right at the intersection and walk to the second traffic light.

This street, which extends from Ueno, is another speciality area, selling Buddhist and Shinto supplies for temples and family altars. When someone dies and the family does not have a Buddhist altar in their house, all they need to do is come here and tell a shop clerk the Buddhist sect to which they belong and the clerk will prepare an altar and its accessories in compli-ance with the specific religious requirements. Small, closet-like family altars, rosaries, and narrow black-and-gold lacquered tablets which serve as nameplates for the dead are sold. Post-humous names are written in gold upon order, and each name-plate will then be placed in the home altar for the bereaved family to pray to.

When you arrive at the second traffic light, turn right and proceed. You will marvel at the host of goods sold in these shops. There is everything from traditional saké bottles to fon-due pots, display cases to candy package paper, or tags saying "Fierce Dog Here" and "Closed Today." The most fascinating items are the colorful plastic food models which look real enough to make your mouth water. A tray of sushi, a bowl of soba, or even a chocolate fudge sundae would be a perfect pop-art gift for a friend back home. In the second block after the next traffic light is **Sogo** 十合, which sells coffee, canned food, nuts etc. At the second traffic light is **Union** ユニオン, specializing in coffee-making equipment; and a few buildings before the second signal, on the other side of the road, is **Kama Asa** 釜浅, selling all kinds of pots and pans.

The name of this area, Kappabashi, comes from a famous bridge which existed in the old days. A legend says that the river under the bridge often flooded in the Edo period causing much trouble to people in the neighborhood and visitors to the Kannon temple. A shopkeeper selling mackintoshes near the bridge (raincoats used to be called *kappa* in old Japanese) resolved to help the people and started a construction project with his own funds. As he began digging and diking, a troop of *kappa* (river imps), came out of the Sumida River to help him. The project was naturally appreciated by many people and the man's business thrived. After his death, neighbors who wanted to share in similar good luck built a shrine along the side of the man's tomb at a nearby temple, and dedicated it to the *kappa* king. The *kappa* shrine is in the compound of **Sogen-ji** 曹源寺 ㊶, four blocks down after you turn left at the traffic light beyond Kama Asa.

The crossing near Union marks the middle of a whole stretch of shops along Kappabashi-dori. Unless you wish to explore the remaining part of the street where there are some more interesting shops selling baskets, lacquerware, etc., turn right at this crossing and walk straight on. Past a traffic light and midway into the next block, there is a *dojō* restaurant, **Iidaya** 飯田屋 ㊷, with an indigo-blue *noren* across its entrance.

Dojō are tiny gray freshwater fish cooked either whole or fillet. The basic dish is *dojō nabe*, which is cooked on a table in a small flat pan with lots of onions. *Yanagawa* (fillets of fish cooked with egg and vegetables) is recommended for the first-timer. Rice and other items must be ordered separately. *(Open 11:00-22:00. Closed on Wednesdays.)*

Farther ahead on the same side of the street is **Imahan** 今半 ㊸, a sukiyaki restaurant—a good place for a quick lunch. Turn right at this crossing to go back to Tawaramachi Station. In the next block after the Sakura Bank is **Miyamoto,** a branch of **Miyamoto Unosuke Shoten** 宮本卯之助商店 ㊹ , a wonderful festival-instruments shop. On the first and second floors, they exhibit and sell *omikoshi, taiko* (drums), and everything needed for a Japanese festival. You are welcome to come in for a close look at the intricate metalwork and smooth lacquered wooden parts of the *omikoshi*. The fourth floor is a unique drum museum called **Taiko-kan** 太鼓館. A rich collection of drums from all over the world is exhibited for visitors to beat and discover different sounds. It is a wonderful place to take children. The drums marked with a red circle on the name plates should not be touched, and those with blue marks should only be tested lightly. To visit this museum, buy a ticket at the counter on the first floor. *(Open 10:00-17:00. Closed on Mondays and Tuesdays.)*

Asakusa wa mainichi omatsuri mitai desu.
(It's like a festival every day in Asakusa.)

NIHOMBASHI

Walking time: 45 minutes

BACKGROUND   Nihombashi, literally "the bridge of Japan," was the proud center of Edo-period Japan. The bridge was built directly beneath Edo Castle, where the shogun lived and from where he ruled the country. At this point, the main overland route between Edo and Kyoto crossed a key waterway used for delivering materials to the castle, as well as various daily necessities to the city center. People and products crossed this bridge from all over the country. Close to the bridge was a large fish market, counted among the three most prosperous business centers in the city. The other two were the Yoshiwara red-light district, and the Kabuki theaters located in adjacent Ningyocho.

GETTING THERE   Take either the Ginza or the Tozai subway lines to Nihombashi and take Exit A1.

Turn right and you will come to a big intersection with Yasuda Trust & Banking Company 安田信託銀行 on the right-hand corner. The road to the left leads to Tokyo Station and is called Sotobori-dori (exterior moat street). Formerly, it was the outer circle of the double trench around Edo Castle. Half of the moat was filled in after World War II. On the other side of Tokyo Station is the Imperial Palace, which stands on the former site

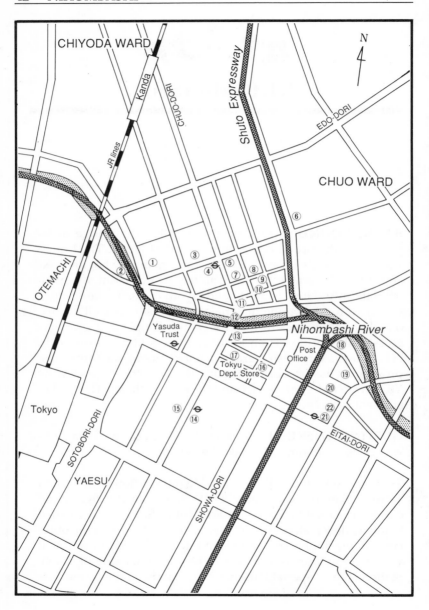

of Edo Castle, surrounded by Uchibori (the inner moat) which still remains after 350 years. The castle's front gate, the Otemon, is located at the end of the road leading straight away from where you are standing. The area between the palace and Tokyo Station is the Marunouchi business district.

Cross the street, turn right, and walk over the bridge spanning the Nihombashi River, named after a famous bridge which spans it. Ahead you can see the classical two-story building of the **Bank of Japan** 日本銀行 ①. At the end of the bridge is another bridge, cross it and walk into **Takiwabashi Park** 常磐橋小公園 ②. This part of the river is a remainder of the exterior moat, and its stone embankment is a relic from the Edo period. High up on this stone wall stands a bronze statue of a man in a frock coat, depicting Eiichi Shibusawa, an acknowledged industrial and financial leader of the early Meiji era. Behind this statue is a neat open space flanked by partially-built stone walls leading to an old-fashioned bridge. This stone structure replaced the original wooden bridge which was built at the time of Ieyasu's official entry into Edo.

Four hundred years ago this place was under the sea, and the extensive area around you, including Nihombashi, Ginza, Yurakucho, and Marunouchi, was marshland. Thus, what is now the heart of Tokyo resulted from a vast civil engineering project.

EDO'S FIRST FINANCIAL CENTER   Ieyasu standardized the monetary system and established institutions for the minting of gold and silver coins. In medieval times, coins from China had been used, and each fief had its own monetary system. Minting coins for national circulation was a revolutionary idea and greatly contributed to the integration and smooth expansion of the economy.

The Bank of Japan, which you see here, is located on the site of the old gold mint. Supervision of the gold coin minting was the privilege of the shogun's most trusted retainer, who was allowed to have his residence right outside the castle's front gate. (The word *ginza* means silver mint, and the first silver mint was built in 1612 in what is now the world-famous Ginza shopping area. A scandal concerning graft caused it to be moved to Ningyocho in 1800.)

Cross the old stone bridge and turn right. Back at the approach of the second bridge, cross the street toward the Bank of Japan. This building is an early Meiji-era masterpiece of Western-style architecture and took from 1890 until 1896 to construct. As you look up from the street, its powerful but elegant design is very impressive. The stately colonnade is softened by the rhythmical repetition of decorative pediments and columns with slight variations in design. The designer and construction supervisor was Dr. Kingo Tatsuno. He was one of the first four students taught by Josiah Conder, a British architect who came to Japan in 1877 and taught Western architecture for forty-four years until his death. Like many other Japanese who pioneered the study of Western science in the early Meiji era, Dr. Tatsuno absorbed classical European taste with great ardor, and this is clearly shown in the style of this building. Beyond the Bank of Japan is another classical edifice, the **Mitsui Main Building** 三井本館 ③, built in 1902. To its right is **Mitsukoshi Department Store** 三越 ④, built in 1914. These two buildings were designed by Tamisuke Yokogawa, one of Dr. Tatsuno's students. The classic European influence is most obvious in the huge fluted columns topped with ornate capitals of the Mitsui Main Building, which now houses the Sakura Bank. The two classical buildings are the heritage of a wealthy family which had its beginning in this area. In Edo-period woodblock prints by Hiroshige and Hokusai, many shops are depicted along this street with Mt. Fuji in the background. A close look at the *noren* of the shops will show that the same crest is used by all of them. This area was the birthplace of the Mitsui zaibatsu and the same crest is still used as the logo for Mitsui companies.

As soon as the reclamation from the sea was completed, Ieyasu encouraged merchants and craftsmen from other parts of the country to come and take up residence here. The most enthusiastic response came from Ise-area merchants. An old book says: "One after another men came and asked for allotments of land on which to live. They took the mud from the excavated moats and laid it over the land which they had been given . . . When houses were built and shop signs were up, as many as half of them read ISE-something."

These Ise merchants developed a system of business strictly controlled by the headquarters in their hometowns. All the employees were people from Ise, who usually started their service as errand boys at the age of ten or so. An employee would be allowed to have a wife when he was about forty, and even then the wife had to stay in Ise where the husband would return for a short time each year. Some of Japan's modern business practices, such as lifetime employment, posting to remote cities without being accompanied by one's family, and the tight control of regional operations by the headquarters, were formed at this time.

The most successful of these Ise merchants was Mitsui Takatoshi who founded Echigoya, a fabric shop which was the predecessor of Mitsukoshi Department Store. Mitsui Bank and Mitsui & Company also developed from Echigoya. These, together with other businesses, grew to form the Mitsui zaibatsu.

Cross the main street toward **Kiya** 木屋 ⑤, a cutlery shop whose red trade mark on its shop signs and windows is taken from the design of old-fashioned U-shaped scissors. Proudly displayed in the windows are original cooking knives made of high-tech steel alloy; they are a bit expensive, but boast durable high cutting quality and are available only at this shop. A short detour from here will take you to **Ozu Paper Museum** 小津和 紙博物館 ⑥, which has an excellent collection of *washi* (Japanese paper), including some rare items. Pass by Kiya's left side, go under the Shuto Expressway, and turn left. The paper dealer's museum is in the basement of the fourth building from the corner, and has a large sign with the kanji 和紙 in front. *(Open 10:00-18:00. Closed on Sundays.)*

Leaving Kiya, turn left, and then left again. Immediately on your left, you will see a large shop sign saying **Isesada** 伊勢定 ⑦, a carry-over from the early Ise merchants, which is a thriving eel restaurant. Beyond the next small crossing on the left is the noodle restaurant **Rikyuan** 利久庵 ⑧, with a stone lantern in front and small bamboo screens covering part of the front wall. Close to the next crossing, on the right, is a slender marker indicating the site of the **Edo fish market** 江戸日本橋小田原町跡 ⑨. Turn right past it.

AN ENGLISH SAMURAI'S RESIDENCE   Around the corner of the second small block on the right is the site of the residence of William Adams, whose story inspired the novel Shogun. Look for a small jewelry shop called **Tagawa Jewels** タガワ宝石店. To the left of this shop, in a small alcove bordered by a low wooden fence, is a stone memorial to **William Adams** ⑩, written in both English and Japanese. William Adams was an Englishman who worked as a pilot on a Dutch ship which was shipwrecked in 1600 off the shore of Kyushu. Ieyasu employed him for his scientific knowledge and expertise in navigation. Adams, who seems to have enjoyed being in the service of the shogun, was given the Japanese name Miura Anjin, derived from the Miura Peninsula where Adams had received a fief from Ieyasu and an old Japanese word meaning "pilot," which was his profession. He married a Japanese woman and died in 1620 in Hirado.

From Adams' memorial, walk straight on to return to the main road, where you should turn left. On this corner is **Yagicho** 八木長 ⑪, dealing in dried bonito, a tradition dating from the Edo period. Other shops nearby also specialize in *nori* (seaweed) and other marine products which are widely used in local delicacies.

OLD FISH MARKET   You have now covered the main part of the former Edo fish market, the prosperity of which is depicted in old woodblock prints and writings. The market existed here until the Great Kanto Earthquake of 1923, which occasioned its move to Tsukiji.

The fishermen had to be licensed by the shogunate to operate here, and the first such privileged group were proud villagers invited by Ieyasu from Osaka. Eventually, this market catered to the city's population of over one million. A *senryū* (humorous short poem) in the haiku style, mentions the fish market as one of the three biggest money-making areas of Edo, each taking in 1,000 *ryō* in gold coins every day. Money would be spent in the morning at the fish market, during the daytime at Kabuki theaters, and at night in the Yoshiwara red-light district. In those days 1,000 *ryō* was a fortune—even more than the carpenters, who were the highest paid wage earners, received in their lifetimes. Of the various kinds of fish, bonito were the most prized. In early summer when the fish were in season, Edo people competed to get a taste of the first catch of the year. According to many *senryū* of the time, these bonito seem to have been a source of argument between husbands and wives; the husband wanting to eat the fish out of vanity, and the wife not wanting to spend a lot of money on a mere fish. The bonito were certainly expensive, especially if they were from the first catch of the year. According to the record of March 25, 1812, seventeen bonito were registered at the fish market as the year's first catch. Of these, six were taken by the shogunate, and three were bought by a high-class restaurant at 2.1 *ryō* each (1 *ryō* is equivalent to approximately ¥70,000). Eight went to a fishmonger who sold one of them to a famous Kabuki actor for 3 *ryō*. When the actor treated the minor actors under him to bonito sashimi, he made big news because of his generosity.

EDO'S NUMBER ONE BRIDGE The large decorative bridge ahead is **Nihombashi** 日本橋 ⑫, spanning the Nihombashi River. Stop just before the bridge and look up at the expressway. A panel set on the recently refurbished side of the elevated motorway reads "Nihombashi." The characters are based on the calligraphy of the last shogun, Yoshinobu. It is a

pity that the expressway dwarfs the beautiful bridge underneath. At the other side of the approach is a tall, black iron pole
with several lamps, which marks the bridge as the starting
point of all roads in Japan.

The Nihombashi bridge was first built in 1603, the year
Ieyasu founded the Tokugawa Shogunate and proclaimed Edo
the new capital of Japan. One year later, the bridge was designated as the starting point of the highway network which
stretched out in four directions and covered all major parts of
the country. This was yet another of Ieyasu's great accomplish-
ments, breaking away from the centuries-long tradition of
treating Kyoto as the national center. Along the highways, stations were built to provide food, horses, and overnight lodg-
ings for travelers. When it became obligatory in 1635 for all the
feudal lords to spend each alternate year in Edo, these highway
stations thrived on the large groups of samurai traveling between Edo and their provinces. The well-equipped infrastruc-
ture for traveling also created a tourism boom among the
commoners. The Nihombashi bridge thus became a pivot
around which all kinds of economic and cultural activities
briskly developed.

The high prestige of Nihombashi, however, began to be
eroded after the Meiji Restoration. The introduction of the railway in the late nineteenth century diminished the importance
of waterway transportation and walking tours. As time passed,
the area continued to be a good shopping center, and the local
merchants' pride is well reflected in the current stone and
metal bridge which was built in 1911, utilizing the best talents
of the time in design and craftsmanship. Then, World War II
broke out, and drastic changes ensued in postwar lifestyles.
The proliferation of cars in everyday life dealt a particularly
bitter blow to the bridge. In the construction rush for the Tokyo
Olympic Games in 1964, a network of expressways was constructed. The space above rivers was used because rivers are
public properties free from the need to negotiate for lease. Per-
sistent appeals by local residents and companies for restoration

of even part of the charm and dignity of the bridge have led to a refurbishment project. In commemoration of the eightieth anniversary of the current bridge in 1991, the four corners at both ends of the bridge were made into small parks with benches and steps for visitors to relax. The bottoms of the terraces are designed to facilitate a better view of the bridge.

Now cross the bridge. There is one more monument on the right side, giving historical information about the bridge. A relief shows the bridge in its old wooden form. Public announcements and other information were once posted on boards here. For instance, when the forty-seven samurai were sentenced to death (see page 133), the announcement was posted here; it was, however, immediately torn down by the infuriated citizens who were sympathetic to the loyal samurai and hoped that their act of revenge would be forgiven.

Walk over to the dark-brown building of **Nomura Securities Co.** 野村証券 ⑬, Japan's largest brokerage house. To its right is a bedding and interior-fabric supplier, **Nishikawa** 西川, which was founded by a family of Omi merchants dealing in cotton fabric. The area this side of the bridge was allotted to immigrants from Omi on Lake Biwa, and the founder of the next store, which is now the Tokyu Department Store, was also from Omi. Still farther along the main road are **Takashimaya** 高島屋 ⑭, an elegant department store, and a book store, **Maruzen** 丸善 ⑮. The second floor of Maruzen specializes in publications in foreign languages, and the fourth floor has a craft center.

For now, however, walk straight on, passing by the right side of Nomura Securities. You will be walking parallel to the Nihombashi River. If you turn right just before the end of the Nomura building, you will find **Taimeiken** restaurant たいめいけん ⑯, in the third block on the left. This restaurant is one of the oldest Western-style restaurants in Tokyo and continues to attract customers with its simple but tasty food. *(Open 10:00-21:00. Closed on Sundays and national holidays.)* A little off to the right past Taimeiken is a good tempura restaurant, **Benkei** 弁

慶 ⑰. *(Open 11:15-14:00, 17:00-21:30. Closed Sunday and national holidays. Tel: 3271-2811.)* Next to it, **Sasa** 笹 is another small but good restaurant serving sushi and *kaiseki. (Opening hours approximately the same as Benkei. Tel: 3271-9950.)*

Taimeiken is also famous for an attached kite museum on the fifth floor. In 1977, the late Shingo Motegi, who founded this restaurant after years of hard apprenticeship, began collecting kites—a tradition on decline. His dedicated efforts have led to a rich collection and revived people's interest in the simple craft. Take the elevator to the fifth floor and step out into a colorful world of fun and fantasy. *(Open 10:00-17:00. Closed on Sundays and national holidays. A small entrance fee is charged.)*

Leaving Taimeiken, turn right and walk straight to the T-junction, where you should turn right again. On your left is the Nomura building. At the next major intersection, where a ramp leads up to the Shuto Expressway on the left, cross the street by the pedestrian bridge and walk toward the square gray building of Nihombashi Post Office, which has a rising sun flag on the roof. The post office stands on the site of the first central post office in Japan.

In the Edo period mail was delivered by messengers. A professional service for official use only used relay runners who were stationed along the highways. Like an ambulance car, they dashed on, signaling their approach by a large lantern and bells attached to the message case. Even the strongest team of men, running without pause, took three days to cover the distance between Edo and Osaka.

TOKYO'S "WALL STREET"   As you go straight, walking by the left side of the post office building, give a glance to the right at its back. Many vertical signboards on the office buildings along this street contain the two kanji for securities (証券) at their bottom. This is because you have just entered Tokyo's "Wall Street." Going under the Shuto Expressway, immediately on the left, you will find a tiny shrine squeezed underneath the motorway; called **Kabuto-jinja** 兜神社 ⑱, or "war helmet shrine," it is related to a famous eleventh-century warrior who reportedly gave his helmet in homage to the Dragon God in the river. As this area has become the center for brokerage houses around the Tokyo Stock Exchange, it is known by the alias of Kabutocho. The massive white building on the right is the **Tokyo Stock Exchange** 東京証券取引所 ⑲.

Walk over to the Tokyo Stock Exchange and bear left to come to the front. However, if you are interested in observing the trading sessions, the visitors' entrance is to the right, accessible by climbing some steps. Admission is free, and the procedure is simple: just fill out a form at the reception desk. *(Open 9:00-16:00, Monday through Friday, except national holidays and the year-end and the New Year vacation. Foreign language commentary is available on telephones.)*

During the Edo period, the river was alive with hundreds of boats which were busy constantly transporting food, fuel, fabric, and just about everything needed to support the life of over one million people. The goods came mostly from Osaka on large vessels which were anchored in Edo Bay. The thriving shipping business was managed by a union of agents who organized themselves into ten subdivisions according to the kind of merchandise handled. By the end of the Edo period, the union had grown to sixty-five groups with over 1,900 dealers, 81 percent of whom were based in the Nihombashi and adjacent Kyobashi areas. This extensive and vigorous system of transportation provided the basis for business plans in the early Meiji era. The Mitsuis moved fast to build a bank in this area, which Shibusawa took over and opened as the Daiichi Bank, the predecessor of the present Dai-Ichi Kangyo Bank. The Iwasakis founded a strong shipping company which was also the initial business of the Mitsubishi financial empire. Just as Lloyd's of London evolved from Lloyd's Coffee House on the Thames River in the seventeenth century, insurance agents too gathered here to become what are now known as Tokyo Marine and Fire Insurance Company and Meiji Life Insurance

Company. When the Bankers' Association, the Chamber of Commerce, a newspaper company, a stock exchange, and trading firms were created one after another in the dozen years after the Meiji Restoration, this area seemed to be perfectly set for its growth according to Shibusawa's plan.

A turnabout came abruptly in 1890 when the Meiji Government offered the Marunouchi area for sale, and the Iwasakis snatched it up, notwithstanding Shibusawa's plea to buy it along with other businessmen. Shipping was soon to be replaced by railway as the means of transport in Japan's industrialized economy. With the opening of Tokyo Station in 1914, Marunouchi emerged as a new business center, draining away business institutions from Kabutocho. However, the stock exchange remained and has become the core of Tokyo's stock market.

Now walk back to the front of the stock exchange. The towering edifice, completed in May 1988, symbolizes Japan's postwar economic miracle and the leaps-and-bounds growth of the stock market. To cope with modern electronic trading and huge volumes of transactions, the stock exchange spent five-and-a-half years and a generous amount of money on renovating its facilities. Along with London and New York, Tokyo is now one of the largest financial centers of the world.

From the stock exchange, walk opposite to the bridge. At the first traffic light turn right for a look at the **site of the first bank in Japan** 銀行発祥の地 ⑳, which is now used as the Kabutocho Branch of the Dai-Ichi Kangyo Bank. Notice the bronze plaque set in the wall of the bank underneath a clock. The unique design, combining the images of a European castle and a five-story pagoda, seems to convey the aspirations of the nineteenth-century Japanese leaders to blend Japanese and European traditions.

Continuing along the main road, you will come to a large intersection. The black building on the right-hand corner is Yamatane Securities which houses **Yamatane Art Museum** 山種美術館 ㉑, known for its fine collection of contemporary

Japanese paintings. To visit, take the elevator up to the ninth floor. *(Open 10:30-17:00. Closed on Mondays.)* The collection includes works by top-class artists such as Taikan Yokoyama, Kokei Kobayashi, Meiji Hashimoto, and Gyoshu Hayami. Being a private collection, it is not large, consisting of only four or five rooms on the eighth and ninth floors of the building, but the serenity of the museum mirrors the refined elegance of the collected works. Its highly tasteful interior, which was designed by Yoshiro Taniguchi, and serene atmosphere are in sharp contrast to the cutthroat competitive business world outside.

As you exit the museum, the Kayabacho Station on the Tozai and Hibiya lines is immediately in front. If you are looking for a place to relax before going home, there is a coffee shop, **Fuji** ㉒, at the corner of the next small block behind the Yamatane Building.

Nihombashi wa yūmei desu.
(Nihombashi is famous.)

NINGYOCHO

Walking time: about 1 hour

BACKGROUND   Ningyocho is a lovely little town which retains much of the cozy atmosphere it had in the Edo period. Its name literally means "doll town" and comes from the local tradition of puppetry as well as from the many doll shops in the district. Formerly a part of Nihombashi, Ningyocho developed into a pleasure district adjacent to the busy business sections near the great Nihombashi bridge. The pleasures included the Yoshiwara red-light district and Kabuki theaters. The Yoshiwara was later moved farther north, but Kabuki theaters continued here for about two hundred years. The many shops dealing in kimono and accessories, as well as other shops selling charmingly designed gift items, developed from the numerous shops which catered to the theatergoers and Kabuki actors who lived in this area. The shops and restaurants are mostly small, family-run establishments, and seem to be proud of their modest size. Here and there, little shrines are still embedded between ordinary houses, receiving intimate attention as though they were beloved neighbors.

GETTING THERE   If you take the Hibiya Line from the direction of the Ginza, try to get on the last car. At Ningyocho Station, take the stairway closest to the rear of the train. After passing through the ticket gate, turn left to come out on the

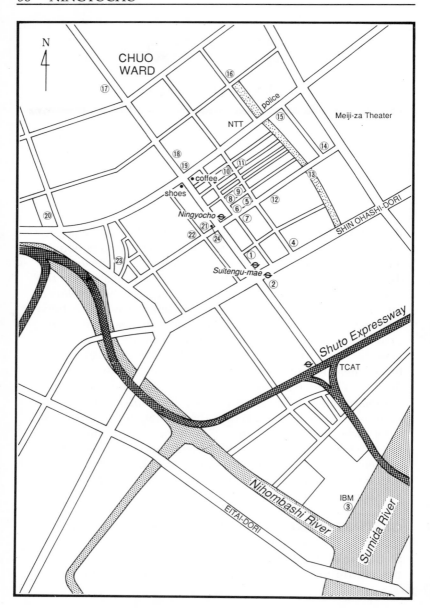

street. Walk left from the exit. If you take the Asakusa Line, the exit comes out at a major intersection. Look for a brown coffee shop, called **Cafe Terrace** ワコー on a corner of the intersection with a men's clothing shop and a book store next to it. Walk straight past the book store and you will see the Hibiya Line exit mentioned earlier. Those taking the recently extended Hanzomon Line should get off at Suitengu-mae, the line's terminal, and then take Exit 7. At street level, turn right. You can also take Exit 5 to come out on the same corner as Suitengu shrine.

As you start walking down this street toward the next major intersection, you will notice several dress shops exhibiting maternity wear. This is because Suitengu shrine, which you are heading for, is associated with childbirth. You will also find Japanese sweet shops displaying seasonal confectioneries, and shops selling pretty cups and bowls. One small sweet shop, **Kotobukido** 寿堂 ①, at the third small crossing from the Hibiya Line exit, sells pretty cakes. *Koganeimo* is a particularly delicious cake sold here; when you unwrap its yellow package, you will find a miniature baked sweet-potato flavored with cinnamon. Another shop ahead on the major intersection sells Japanese-style cookies and *ningyō-yaki* (waffles filled with sweet bean-paste and molded into dolls' faces). The *shiso*-flavored cookies are good.

SUITENGU SHRINE   Beyond a grove of trees at the intersection is **Suitengu** 水天宮 ② . There is a stairway leading from the street to the shrine. Two bronze lanterns in front of the main building are decorated with dragons and water designs. Near the left-hand lantern are two iron anchors. These symbols are related to water and represent the origin of the shrine.

Suitengu has a sad story behind its founding. It is a branch of Suitengu in Kurume, Kyushu, which is said to have been founded after the historic defeat of the Heike clan at the Battle of Dannoura in the twelfth century. Their supporters having been defeated, the six-year-old Emperor Antoku and his mother plunged themselves into the sea carrying with them the sacred sword, one of the three imperial treasures symbolizing legitimacy to the throne. They planned to take it to a palace which they believed existed at the bottom of the sea. One of the court ladies fled to Kurume and built a shrine to pray for the repose of their souls. She named the shrine Suitengu (celestial palace in the sea). The combined association of a child emperor and water gave the shrine its connection with pregnancy and birth. Nowadays, the shrine is best known as a place to pray for a safe delivery, and you often see expectant mothers or babies carried by their grandmothers worshiping there.

A baby's birth is usually preceded by a prebirth celebration, and a thanksgiving visit to a shrine follows the birth. The prebirth celebration is held on a day in the fifth month of pregnancy when the expectant mother begins to wear a belly band to protect her abdomen. This shrine sells white cotton cloth consecrated at the altar for use as bellybands. The celebrants often visit a shrine like Suitengu to pray for an easy and safe delivery. Ever since the Edo period, the Day of the Dog has been popular for this celebration because dogs bear young easily and all the puppies grow to be strong. The colorful papiermâché dogs which you often see at Japanese craft shops developed from this idea. The naming of the baby usually takes place on the seventh day when there may be a small family celebration. The visit to a shrine is usually on the thirty-second day after the birth of a boy and on the thirty-third day for a girl. Originally, this was the occasion for initiating a newborn baby into the village community under its tutelary god, but nowadays this local custom has been lost and people go to any shrine they like.

Suitengu is also related to Benten, the goddess of music and charm, who is one of the *shichifukujin* (seven lucky gods) in this area. The shrine's *ennichi* (fair day) is celebrated on the fifth of every month, and numerous stalls are set up around the shrine. On May 5 and 6 they celebrate the annual festival with Kagura dances and processions of *omikoshi* and floats. The best time to see the procession is usually between 12:00 and 2:30 P.M.

* * *

SUGGESTED DETOUR: Time and weather permitting, you might enjoy a short detour for a stroll along the Sumida River. Go down to the street by the same stairway and turn left at the bottom toward the Shuto Expressway, and passing underneath it, turn right. You will be close to Exit 2 of Suitengu-mae Station. You can walk underground from Exit 5 mentioned earlier, to Exit 2. Exit 1 is connected to the airline counters of the Tokyo City Air Terminal. Cross the street in front of Exit 2 and bear right toward the square IBM office building soaring ahead. Walk through the IBM premises, passing along the left side of the building. You will come out to a neatly designed **paved walkway on the riverside** ③. With low stairways built in a wavelike pattern and benches placed here and there, the riverside promenade is a good place to relax as you watch boats sailing by. Return by the same route.

* * *

Back at the intersection near Exit 5 of Suitengu-mae Station, cross the street to the cookie shop and turn right. Walk to the next traffic light and turn left. On the right is a small shrine called **Matsushima-jinja** 松島神社 ④. The shrine is related to Daikoku who is the god of five cereals and wealth, and the second of the seven lucky gods in this area. Apparently, this tiny shrine is dedicated to an especially versatile god who is responsive to as many as sixteen different kinds of wishes such as business prosperity, progress in music and other studies, as well as protection from danger. It is also one of the bird shrines which celebrates the Lucky Rake Fair in November. From its well-tended look, there is no denying that the shrine is very much alive in the hearts of the people of the neighborhood.

From Matsushima-jinja, turn right and walk straight until you come to a crossing with traffic lights. Here is a shopping street called Amazake Yokocho lined with numerous interesting shops and eating places.

Cross the street and turn left. A little off the corner is **Shinoda-zushi** 志乃多寿司 ⑤, which sells *inari-zushi* (seasoned rice packed in fried tofu) as well as a variety of rolled sushi. These are for take-out only. Next to it is **Bachiei** ばち英, which has a white shop sign in the shape of the plectrum used for the *shamisen* (three-stringed instrument), indicating the shop's specialty. Beyond it is **Iwaido** 岩井堂 ⑥, custom-making *tsuzura* (boxlike lacquered storage baskets) with a family crest on each. Beyond the small crossing are more shops such as a *soba* restaurant in a weathered wooden building, and shops selling handmade tofu or aromatic tea. Across the street from the front of Iwaido is a popular shop, **Yanagiya** 柳屋 ⑦, often with many people lining up in front. They are waiting to buy fish-shaped waffles called *taiyaki*. *Tai* (sea bream) is considered an auspicious fish in Japan and its shape is often used as a popular design motif.

At the corner of the square basket shop, turn right. Several buildings away is **Imahan** 今半 ⑧, a beef shop with a restaurant on the right. Its lunch time *(11:30-16:00)* provides a good opportunity to sample choice beef at a bargain price. Ask for steak *teishoku* which is available in three classes: A, B, or C, according to the size of the meat. *Kaiseki* lunch is also available in neat tatami-matted rooms upstairs upon reservation *(Tel: 3666-4584)*. Passing Imahan, turn right, and you will find **Homitei** 芳味亭 ⑨ on the right. With its slatted doors and many potted plants in front, it looks like a Japanese restaurant, but it serves good Western-style dishes with Shitamachi flavoring. The tasty hashed beef is recommended. Or, try *yōshoku bentō* (an assortment of hamburger steak, fried shrimp, roast pork, and salad). *(Open 11:00-14:00, 17:00-21:00. Closed on Mondays.)* Past this restaurant is a crossing where if you turn right, you will come back to the Amazake Yokocho shopping street. One block to the left of this crossing on the right-hand side of the street is a good sushi restaurant, **Kizushi** 喜寿司 ⑩. To the right of the crossing next to an office building on the left-hand side of the street is **Suehiro-jinja** 末広神社 ⑪, dedicated to

Bishamon, the god of treasure, who is the third of the seven lucky gods.

Back at Amazake Yokocho, cross the street and turn left. As you walk straight, enjoy looking at the various shops dealing in decorative sushi, *sembei* with many different flavors, and kimono. With the area's historic tradition of catering to the elegant taste of theatergoers, almost everything sold in this town is beautifully designed to please the eyes. On the right-hand side of the street past a *sembei* shop, **Guruton** ぐるとん ⑫ serves simple Western-style lunches and à la carte dinners in the evening. The day's lunches are indicated on a small sign in front, available as A, B, or C set, with a cup of coffee or glass of white wine included in both the A and B sets.

At the next traffic light, cross the street and keep straight. Notice a statue of the Kabuki hero **Benkei** 弁慶 ⑬ in the middle of a wooded pavement sandwiched between car lanes. Surrounded by highrises, this classical statue posing against a wooden gate seems a bit odd at first glance, but it represents the local government's efforts to retain the area's historical identity.

About 350 years ago there was a thriving theater section designated by the shogunate, comprising two small towns called Fukiyacho and Sakaicho (located close to the Ningyocho intersection which you will come to later). The licensed Kabuki theaters Nakamura-za and Ichimura-za were based there, along with several puppet theaters. Numerous puppet craftsmen lived around the theater section making and repairing puppets for the performances. Even after the theater section was moved to Asakusa, the craftsmen continued to live in Ningyocho. The town continued to prosper after the removal of the theater section because of a fashionable entertainment district opened by the Sumida riverside in the Meiji era. The new pleasure district, called Hamacho, was patronized by government and business dignitaries. A large theater, the Meiji-za, was built at the center of the new town and is still in business today.

Cross this intersection and turn left, then right, to reach a dark-red brick building with few windows in its lower stories. This is the Tokyo branch of the **Kurita Museum** 栗田美術館 ⑭ with a collection of excellent old porcelains including Imari, Nabeshima, and Kakiemon wares. The Tokyo branch has only a small part of the fabulous collection of the main museum in Ashikaga City, but is quite interesting. Enter through the glass door and take your shoes off in front of the big golden Kannon statue. Go upstairs to the office on the left where you pay the admission and take a small elevator to the fifth floor which exhibits small items. The fourth floor shows large vases and plates from the seventeenth and eighteenth centuries. *(Open throughout the year, 10:00-17:00, except the last three days of December.)* The main museum is worth a day trip on another occasion. *(Kurita Museum, 1542 Komaba-sho, Ashikaga-shi, Tochigi-ken. Tel: 0284-91-1026.)*

Leaving the museum, backtrack to the traffic light and cross the street halfway for a brief stroll along the wooded pavement to the right. At the end of the walkway bear right to the next traffic light. The fourth of the seven lucky gods, Jurojin, is enshrined at **Kasama Inari-jinja** 笠間稲荷 ⑮, a little off to the right of the lights. Facing the large street with its heavy traffic, the antique-looking shrine seems isolated, but it livens up during the New Year festivities when people visit all seven of the lucky gods.

At this major intersection, cross to the other side toward the police office. Turn left, and at the next traffic light turn right to walk under the archway just before a large NTT building. This area is part of a busy fabric and apparel wholesale section which extends far ahead of you almost to Asakusabashi. At a crossroads past the brown building on the right, walk a short distance ahead to look at a shop on the right with a short brown *noren* ⑯ which specializes in the painting of *mon* (family crests). When people buy materials for formal kimono, they have to arrange to have their specific family crest affixed before the kimono is actually sewn. At this shop you can peep in from the street to observe the way workers confirm details of designs and how they carefully trace according to specification. Several buildings beyond the *mon* workshop are kimono dealers displaying brocade obi and rolls of fabric.

EDO'S FIRST RED-LIGHT DISTRICT   Back at the crossing, turn right and walk straight to the next traffic light. This street is the approximate northern border of the first Yoshiwara, the southern border of which is the present Amazake Yokocho. The word *yoshiwara*, meaning "field of reeds," was derived from the thick growth of reeds in the marshy land which was reclaimed to make way for the licensed red-light district in 1616.

One of the most distinctive features of Edo was its scarcity of women. Censuses of commoners living in Edo always showed the male-female ratio to be about two to one. Since samurai usually left their families at home in the provinces, the overall female ratio among them was even lower. Located close to thriving business areas around Nihombashi, the Yoshiwara enjoyed a booming prosperity until the great fire in 1657 when it was demolished and moved to Asakusa.

This land of pleasure was not merely an assembly of brothels, but rather comprised a fashionable society comparable to that of a royal court. Its courtesans, who were all highly educated in music and literature, felt equal to socializing with daimyo and high-class samurai. Strict rules of etiquette rejected outright demonstration of power and wealth, and people competed in expressing their taste and thoughts in the most sophisticated and eloquent manner.

 When you arrive at a major crossing with a traffic light, your basic direction is to the left. However, if you go right and turn right past the next traffic light and take the first small corner to the left, you will find **Suginomori-jinja** ⑰, the fifth lucky god shrine. This shrine formerly prospered as one of the three lottery-drawing shrines of Edo. Retrace your steps to the first traffic light and walk straight on. You will be walking toward the Ningyocho intersection mentioned at the beginning of this chapter. The right-hand side of this street was the theater district described earlier. On the other side of the street is **Ubukeya** うぶけや ⑱, with wonderful old shop signs above its doorway. The handmade scissors are treasured by enthusiastic customers. Fairly close to the intersection is a pottery shop, **Iseryu** 伊勢竜 ⑲, displaying decorative plates and bowls in the front window.

At the intersection, your direction is straight, however, if you go right you will arrive at Nihombashi in about ten minutes. Just before the Shuto Expressway, the sixth lucky god shrine is located around the corner of the Fuji Bank on the right. This small shrine, **Tokiwa Inari** 常盤稲荷 ⑳, squeezed in between other buildings, is easily missed. To continue, cross the intersection toward a shoe shop and walk straight along the main road. A signpost on the street just in front of the Hibiya Line subway entrance explains that on this side of the street used to be the Kakigaracho Ginza where the silver mint continued in business until 1868.

Around the corner to the right, the conspicuous white-walled building is a chicken restaurant, **Tamahide** 玉ひで ㉑. In the next block, a metal plate on the left-hand side of a driveway leading to an underground garage indicates the site of **Junichiro Tanizaki's birthplace** 谷崎潤一郎 生誕地 ㉒. The famous author of many novels, including *The Makioka Sisters*, was born here in 1883. Because the family business went into bankruptcy when he was a schoolboy, his graduation from primary school was threatened. However, the neighbors who loved the bright boy donated money for his further education. Thus, the great writer owed his later literary success in part to the intimate communal cooperation which characterizes Shitamachi.

Walk a little further and you will come to the seventh of the area's seven lucky gods. Pass the traffic light and turn right at the next corner. Immediately take the next left and a small bronze-roofed shrine will be seen ahead squeezed in among the highrises. **Koami-jinja** 小網神社 ㉓   related to Fukurokuju, the god of wealth and longevity. The shrine is known for its unique five-hundred-year-old festival, Doburoku Matsuri, held on November 27. Kagura dances are performed and *doburoku* (raw saké fermented from the year's first rice harvest) is served to worshipers at noon. May 28 is another festive occasion.

Well, this is the end of today's excursion. If you care to stop for a cup of coffee, try **Kaiseiken** 快生軒 ㉔, an old-fashioned coffee shop near the subway station. Or, if you are hungry, it might be fun to have lunch at Tamahide. This restaurant has continued in business since 1760 and still uses recipes from the Edo period for their chicken dishes. Their *oyako domburi* (chicken and eggs over rice served with a ginger-flavored soup) is a bit sweet, but delicious. *(Open for lunch between 11:30 and 13:00. In the evenings they serve chicken sukiyaki and other chicken dishes. Closed on Sundays and national holidays.)*

> *Sayonara. Mata kono tsugi ne.*
> (Good-bye, until next time.)

KANDA

Walking time
Kanda–Ochanomizu Station: 30 minutes
Ochanomizu–Yushima: 40 minutes
Ochanomizu–Jimbocho: 40 minutes

BACKGROUND "I hear you are an *Edokko*." "I sure am! I was born in Kanda." This proud response has often been cited as evidence that Kanda was the cradle of Edo commoners. The original settlers who came to live here were workers and craftsmen assembled by the Tokugawa Shogunate for the construction of the new capital. Despite priding themselves on their ability as craftsmen, the Edo commoners were both poor managers and propertyless, and thus never rose to influential positions. At times, they even bragged of having few resources. Saving money was regarded as shameful, as depicted in this *senryū* of the period:

"A misborn *Edokko*—
He has accumulated money!"

The excellent location of Kanda has been an important factor in its continuing vitality even up to the present time. Its proximity to the political and economic centers, plus its convenient transportation, have enabled the town to survive successive economic and social changes. The great variety of Kanda is obvious when compared with the more integrated business center of Nihombashi.

GETTING THERE Take the Ginza Line to Kanda Station. At

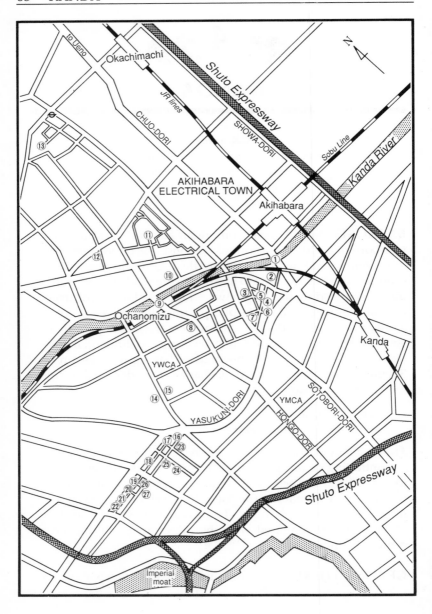

the station, ascend the stairway near the front of the Asakusa-bound train, and take Exit 6.

Along the underground passageway of the station stand a number of old-fashioned shops including a barber, tailor, and shoe dealer. These are the remains of Japan's very first underground shopping center, opened in 1932. Cross the large street in front of the exit, turn right, and walk straight ahead. This busy street connects Nihombashi behind you with Ueno ahead, and has been an important main thoroughfare since the Edo period. Passing the railway overpass, you will come to an old concrete bridge with four corner pillars, each with anti-quated lamps. This bridge, **Manseibashi** 万世橋 ①, spans the Kanda River, which used to form part of the exterior moat of Edo Castle. Beyond the bridge is the famous Akihabara shopping center for electric appliances. For now, however, turn around to look back the way you came.

When Ieyasu became the national ruler and started his fabulous city construction in 1603, there was a plateau extending like a peninsula behind you on the right. The Kanda River did not exist then, as it is really a canal cut later. A vast marsh dotted with a few small isles lay spread ahead of you. In order to implement his city plan, Ieyasu reclaimed the land with soil dug out from part of the plateau. The scraped-out site of the plateau was given to construction workers, craftsmen, and greengrocers. They lived in groups by trade, and the towns were named after their vocations, such as carpenter, plasterer, blacksmith, dyer, and candle maker. Some of these names are still retained in areas near the JR Kanda Station, although very few of these businesses remain, having long since been displaced by modern offices.

Like Nihombashi, Manseibashi was built at the junction of a busy waterway and land route. After the Edo period, another level of crossroads was constructed here—the railroads supported by the beautiful brick walls seen to the right. To accommodate bustling passengers and cargoes transported from four directions, the JR Akihabara Station was designed in the form of a cross. There was another smaller but older station standing by this bridge; however, it was closed and has now been turned into a railway museum.

Let's visit this railway museum, which is now called the **Transportation Museum** 交通博物館 ②, with recently added displays of cars and airplanes. Walk back to the railway over-pass under which you came and turn right. Immediately on the right the streamlined blue-and-white front of a *shinkansen* train and a classical black steam-locomotive will catch your eye. The first floor is used to exhibit old trains, the inner workings of train engines, and a panoramic model landscape to show train operations using miniatures. The most popular display is the simulator for driving a train, which combines audio, visual, and mechanical devices to create a very real feeling of operat-ing a train. The theme of the second-floor display is automo-biles, and the third floor, aviation. On the patio outside are charming late nineteenth-century steam engines imported from England and America. (*Open 9:00-16:00. Closed on Mon-days.*)

Leaving the museum, turn right and then right again, and walk towards the elevated railway. At the end of the brick wall turn right for a look at the **Shoheibashi** bridge which has been on this site since the early seventeenth century, and which used to be frequented by elite young samurai who went to the sho-gunate academy near here. The current bridge was built in 1927. Local residents, regretting the postwar lackluster image of the historic bridge, pushed the relevant authorities for refur-bishment; the metal partitions and pavement are the results of their efforts.

Retrace your steps to the brick wall and cross the street. Turn left and take the first right to **Yabusoba** やぶそば ③, a famous *soba* restaurant situated in a walled-in compound. Cus-tomers come in a constant stream, lured by the hand-rolled, slightly greenish buckwheat noodles made here. One helping of noodles is rather light for a meal, and many people order two *seiro* (cold noodles with sauce on the side). An English menu is available. Leaving Yabusoba, take the narrow lane ahead. A relatively large traditional building at the next crossing is **Botan** ぼたん ④, specializing in chicken sukiyaki. The restaurant has the wonderful atmosphere of prewar Tokyo. Ask for *torisuki. (Open 12:00-20:00. Closed on Sundays and national holidays. For reservation, call 3251-0577.)*

To the left of the crossing are two traditional wooden buildings. On the left is **Takemura** 竹むら ⑤ which sells *agemanjū* (deep-fried sweet dumplings). This beautiful prewar wooden house escaped the air raids during World War II, and its exterior and interior designs should be of great interest to lovers of Japanese architecture. Opposite this shop is **Isegen** いせ源, a fish restaurant known for its *ankō* (angler) during the winter months when the fish is in season. Back at Botan, turn left and then right at a T-junction. Several buildings ahead is **Matsuya** まつや ⑥, another good *soba* restaurant. Two large paper lanterns are hung high on the facade. More casual than Yabusoba, Matsuya is patronized by *soba* lovers who believe simple service is perfect for this plain food. You might enjoy *mori* (cold *soba*) or *goma soba* which uses sesame as an ingredient. In the winter, hot, curry-flavored *karē namban* is a treat. They also serve *tendon.*

Leaving Matsuya, turn right and then right again at the next traffic light. You may keep going straight from Matsuya to reach the Jimbocho bookstore section described later. After turning right, however, walk a couple of short blocks to the next traffic light. Near the light is **Omiya** 近江屋 ⑦ bakery. In the back of the clean, spacious, high-ceilinged shop is a lounge where customers can help themselves to as many cups of coffee, orange juice, or milk as they like after the first paid cup. Pay at the counter to receive a plastic cup. *(Open 9:00-18:30. Closed on Sundays and national holidays.)*

To continue, cross the main street at the nearby traffic light and walk up the hill ahead. This ascending slope, which is short but rather steep, gives an idea of the height of the plateau mentioned earlier. Thus far you have walked through the leveled lowland and are now going up to the remaining part of the plateau. The area at the top is called Surugacho, so named because it was given to Shogun Ieyasu's most devoted military men from Suruga, Ieyasu's hometown. Halfway up the hill, turn right around the corner of the park and take the first left, passing by an old building on stone walls. A little surprise awaits you at the top of the hill where an old cathedral emerges on elevated ground on the other side of the street. Its complex contours contrast sharply against the straight lines of the modern buildings around. It is the Resurrection Cathedral of the Orthodox Church of Japan, popularly known as **Nikoraido** ニ コライ堂 ⑧ after Archbishop Nikolai, who administered it from 1861 until his death in 1912. This is the largest example of Byzantine architecture in Japan. The original plan was drawn by M.A. Shchurpov, a Russian architect in St. Petersburg, and Josiah Conder adapted it for this site. The construction was supervised by Conder and took eight years to complete, from 1884–1892. The bell tower has six bells of different sizes and tone, which are rung twice on Sundays. Their melodious sound, the ting-a-ling of the smaller bells mixed with the deep bong of the big bell, used to echo all over the Surugacho area everyday, enhancing the area's exotic atmosphere after the Meiji Restoration.

From here, you have two alternatives: either go right to Yushima where you can see shrines popular since the Edo period, or left to Jimbocho, a bustling bookstore district.

YUSHIMA ROUTE

Leaving the cathedral, return to the main road and turn left. The brown and beige highrise building on the left has some restaurants, stores, and restrooms in its basement. It is also connected to Shin-Ochanomizu subway station. The JR Ochanomizu Station beyond is always bustling with students. The name of the station, as well as the surrounding area, comes from a spring of good water *(mizu)* which used to flow here and was used for preparing green tea *(ocha)*. Now Ochanomizu is a students' town with nearly thirty educational institutions including universities, high schools, and vocational schools.

To the right of the station is a big bridge called **Hijiribashi** 聖橋 ⑨. As you look down to the Kanda River from the right side of the bridge, you can see the JR station, and the Marunouchi Line subway trains as they emerge briefly from underground. On a higher mound to the left, the steep bronze roof of **Yushima Seido** 湯島聖堂 ⑩ can be seen. This large shrine is your next destination, but to get there, you must cross the bridge along its left side and turn left at the other end of the bridge. Descending the stairway to the street, turn left at the bottom to reach the front gate of the shrine. Once in the compound, pass under another gate to the left. Here is a large bronze statue of Confucius, because this shrine is dedicated to the Chinese philosopher whose teachings provided the intellectual foundation of Tokugawa feudalism. Proceeding further to the back of the compound, you will come to the main building, cloaked in austere silence. On top of the grand roof are some devilish black animal gods, looking as if they had just slid down the steep slope to halt your further approach to the sacred hall.

The main building is a replica of the original which was lost in the air raids during World War II. The washstand and the lacquered gate near it have been retained from the eighteenth century. Actually, the Confucian shrine is the only surviving part of the school founded by the fifth shogun to teach Confucianism to the sons of his retainers, who were required to earn its diploma in order to qualify as legitimate successors of their families.

Leaving the shrine from the front gate, walk around the block to the back of the shrine. Ahead is an intersection where you should make a U-turn to visit the next shrine, **Kanda Myojin** 神田明神 ⑪. A small, pretty shop at the entrance of the shrine is **Amanoya** 天野屋 , which sells products using rice malt such as miso and *amazake* (a sweet drink made from fermented rice), as well as *nattō* (fermented soy beans).

Passing another gate with guardian gods in its side sections, you will see a Kagura dance stage on the right which was donated by the late Konosuke Matsushita, the founder of the Matsushita Electric Industrial Company. Before proceeding to the main building, take a look at a steep stone stairway behind the Kagura stage. The straight drop shows the height of the plateau. It also gave rise to the popular name of the stairway, *otoko-zaka* (male slope). Standing on the top, one can imagine how the geographical advantage of this spot was appreciated by many people—visitors who praised the excellent views, or Edo-bound sailors in the faraway bay who could recognize the soaring ginkgo trees which used to stand here. One of the large trees remains by the stairway, and more grow in the back of the compound.

As you return to the main building, notice a mound of rocks with a pair of stone lions. The **lion mountain** was built in 1990 in celebration of the emperor's enthronement. The lions, however, date from 1716 and are the work of an expert stone carver of the time. He produced three pairs of stone lions in a display based on a popular saying that lions are brave enough to kick their baby off a sheer precipice in order to test its strength.

Kanda Myojin is related to Taira no Masakado, a fierce tenth-century warrior from the Kanto area, who tried to build his own empire in defiance of the emperor in Kyoto. In the course of the bloody wars against his kin, he was captured and beheaded at a place in northern Kanto. It is said that the moment his head was cut off, it rose into the air and flew as far as Edo, landing in what is now Otemachi. Awed by his tremendous power, people buried the head where it fell and built a shrine. On the site stands a monument called the Kubizuka, squeezed between the highrises of the Long-Term Credit Bank of Japan and Mitsui & Company.

Always the tactful politician, Ieyasu naturally noticed the shrine's popularity among the original inhabitants of Edo and proclaimed the shrine to be the guardian of all the people of the new city. However, he needed the shrine's original site for expanding his castle, so he moved it to the current location. The shrine's festival in mid-May is a big, bustling affair with a full-scale celebration taking place every other year. *(For information, call 3254-0753.)*

In the twentieth century, the shrine and its neighborhood were used for the setting of a very popular detective novel written by Kodo Nomura. The hero, Boss Heiji, lived with his beloved wife in a humble house somewhere underneath the steep stairway. He was a plainclothes man working for the shogunate along with his overanxious, hasty assistant, Hachigoro. Boss Heiji captured the hearts of many readers, even intellectuals, because of his dashing demeanor and his ability to arrive at clear-cut, yet humane solutions. More than four-hundred sequels of the story won fame and fortune not only for the author, but for the publishers and TV stations which dramatized it. After the author's death, a stone monument in memory of Boss Heiji was erected here on the right of the main building. The donors did not forget to give a memorial to Hachigoro, too, smaller, but made of the same green stone as the one used for his boss.

Proceeding from Boss Heiji's memorial, turn left and then right to exit from the back gate of the shrine. Descend the steps, and at the street level, turn left to walk toward a major intersection with a traffic light. Your direction is to the right at the intersection, but a short detour straight ahead will take you to **Kobayashi** 小林 ⑫, specializing in *washi*. Pass another traffic light and look for the words "Origami Kaikan" on the wall of a six-story concrete building on the left. A *noren* above a short flight of steps marks the entrance to the shop. Kits and specimens of various crafts made with printed or colored paper stimulate the imagination. Lessons are given in a classroom on the sixth floor at reasonable fees. *(For information, call 3811-4025. Open 9:00-17:00. Closed on Sundays and holidays.)*

Return to the major intersection, turn left, and walk straight for about five minutes to your last destination, **Yushima Tenjin** 湯島天神 ⑬, at the end of the gentle rise. It also has a long history, existing here even before Edo became the capital of Japan. Interestingly, the basic layout of this shrine is very similar to that of Kanda Myojin. Here, too, you can see a Kagura dance stage on the right of the compound, and a steep male stairway on the right of the main building. A feature of this shrine is its profusion of *ema* (wooden prayer tablets with paintings of the animal of the year). The wooden tablets are hung on frames all over the compound by students who wish for success in their school entrance exams, as the god of this shrine is believed to assist scholarly progress.

Yushima Tenjin is one of the famous Tenjin shrines related to Sugawara Michizane, an outstanding scholar and poet of the Heian period who was employed by the emperor in high positions, but was falsely accused of plotting treason. Although Sugawara was innocent, he was exiled to Dazaifu in Kyushu, where he died two years later, lonely and destitute. Shortly after his death, disasters followed one after another in Kyoto. The citizens were horrified and believed that they were being cursed by the vengeful spirit of the unfortunate Sugawara and erected a shrine in order to calm his soul. The deified Sugawara was called Tenjin, which literally means the god of heaven. When the disasters stopped, people remembered Sugawara's remarkable literary talents and came to visit the shrine to pray for progress in scholarship and literary arts. Sugawara's story was adopted in both Bunraku and Kabuki plays, creating long-lived classics.

Because of Sugawara's great love for plum blossoms, Tenjin shrines often have many plum trees in the compound, and their emblems are all the same—a plum flower with five petals. In the twentieth century, this particular shrine with its white plums was used as the setting for a tragic love story in which the lovers had their last secret meeting here, when the white plums, symbolizing the heroine's noble character, were in full bloom. The beautiful curved bridge connecting the main building with an attached hall on the left was also used in the stage set.

February 25 is Sugawara's anniversary, and the celebration at this shrine continues from February 15 until the middle of March when the plum blossoms are in bloom. Special programs during this period include tea ceremony and traditional performing arts, such as *Tenjin daiko* (drum performance).

Descend the stairway to the street, either by the straight "male slope" or by the "female slope" to its left. The area at the bottom of the stairway at one time prospered as a red-light district, and several traditional buildings remain from prewar years. Turn left and then right to come to a major intersection, on both sides of which are the entrances to Yushima Station on the Chiyoda Line.

JIMBOCHO ROUTE

Leaving the Orthodox Church, turn left and left again, then take the first right. This short street is lined with medical facilities. At the main street, turn left and walk straight on. Though not visible from the street, the YWCA is a little off to the left. The YMCA and the Salvation Army also have their headquarters not very far from here. Close to the YWCA is the original site of Chuo University, which has since moved out to the suburbs. On the other side of the main street are the graduate schools of Meiji University, including the classical domed building of the **Faculty of Law** 明治大学法学部 ⑭, built in 1886. These are leading private universities with long histories dating back to the period shortly after the Meiji Restoration.

When its 280-year-long isolation ended, Japan entered into commerical treaties with the Western powers. The tough trade and diplomatic conditions imposed by Western nations created a tremendous demand for legal experts. Many law schools were founded to fill the needs, and they became the great universities such as those mentioned here. Recently the explosive increase in the number of students has compelled these schools to move to the suburbs where they can afford larger campuses and better facilities.

Facing the classical building of the law school is **Ochano-mizu Square** お茶の水スクェア ⑮, a rare example of the successful refurbishment of a Tokyo landmark, completed in 1987. Architect Arata Isozaki renovated the 62-year-old buildings of Shufunotomo Company, designed by an American architect, and blended it with a modern highrise of his own design to create a mix of pre- and postwar modernism. One of the serious obstacles to the refurbishment was the terracotta relief ornaments on the walls; seldom used in postwar architecture, the technique of making them had died out. After extensive search, an old Shigaraki potter was found who vaguely remembered how to make them, and he reproduced the beige reliefs with motifs of books, torches, plants, and vases. The refurbishment naturally received the warm support of the area's longtime residents, who anxiously watched the progress of the project which was "like reforming an old tailored-jacket, keeping the sleeves and sewing them onto a body of modern design and materials," according to a tailor, a longtime resident.

The left-hand part of the building is the Casals Hall, which hosts chamber music. Nearby are **Merrel,** a chic Western-style restaurant, and **Café Molina.** *(Open throughout the year; the restaurant, 11:00–18:00, and the coffee shop, 10:30–20:00.)*

Leaving Ochanomizu Square, turn left. You may have noticed many music shops along the way, and you will see more as you proceed. Numerous sports shops and travel agents also thrive in this area. Indeed, these leisure industries were quick to invade this college and bookstore district, reflecting the primary concerns of today's students. However, the publishing and book distribution industries which grew with the rise of the universities are still firmly anchored in sections to your right and straight ahead. In terms of the number of publishers, as many as 80 percent of the country's total are concentrated in Tokyo, and 60 percent are in the Kanda area. One of the leading publishers, **Sanseido** 三省堂 ⑯, publishing since 1881, is lo-

cated on the other side of the next major intersection. At the
traffic light, cross the street to the right and then over to the
other side toward the eight-story Sanseido building. From
here, you can either walk along the main street, Yasukuni-dori,
or take a smaller street which runs parallel to it. Either way,
you will come to the same subway station, Jimbocho.

If you opt for the main road, turn right at the front of
Sanseido. Several blocks ahead is the hub of the used book
business in Tokyo. The majority of stores along the main street
have long been based here, and the dedicated proprietors are
eagerly seeking ways of continuing their traditional business.
A few buildings away from Sanseido is **Ohya Shobo** 大屋書房
⑰, exhibiting old woodblock prints in the display window. In
the third block, next to a bookstore called Matsumura which
sells large-sized art books, is **Isseido** 一誠堂 ⑱, the cradle of
secondhand bookstores in this area. Beyond the intersection
with traffic lights is a nine-story building where a branch of the
Dai-Ichi Kangyo Bank operates in the lower stories. On the top
floor is a unique movie theater, the Iwanami Hall, which specializes in films produced by small production companies of
various countries. A little beyond it, a dark-brown building
with a see-through elevator shaft is the **Kosho Center** 古書セン
ター ⑲, housing several bookstores. Notice a number of old
Noh masks displayed in shelves near the elevator. Next to this
building is **Hara Shobo** 原書房 ⑳, selling ukiyo-e reprints and
books related to ukiyo-e on the second floor. In the middle of
the next block, **Toyoda Shobo** 豊田書房 ㉑ specializes in books
on Kabuki and other traditional performing arts. Further beyond is **Kitazawa Bookstore** 北沢書店 ㉒ with two beautiful
marble columns in front. The store carries many foreign books,
some very rare ones. The entrance to Jimbocho Station on the
Hanzomon and Toei Shinjuku lines is nearby.

Those of you who like back streets should turn left at
Sanseido. On the left stands a silver-colored arch utilizing lilies
of the valley as a design; walk under it. Small shops in various
trades mix with bookstores, creating a pleasant shopping

center. Next to an antique shop on the left is **Hachimaki** はちま
き ㉓, a tempura restaurant. Take the second left from this
small restaurant, and you will find a large coffee shop,
Renoire, on the right, and in the next small block, **Candle** きゃ
んどる ㉔, also on the right. A wooden latticed window and a
signboard in front mark the entrance to this tiny coffee shop
tended by a gentle gray-haired lady. The atmosphere is like
that of a secret place in a fairy tale, where time has stopped.

Back at the shopping street, turn left, passing **Uchiyama
Shoten** 内山書店 ㉕, founded by a Japanese family dedicated
to the promotion of friendship between China and Japan since
prewar years. Across the street from Uchiyama is another
bookstore, **Toho Shoten** 東方書店, specializing in books on
China. Beyond the traffic light, the shopping street continues.
The Salvation Army stands on the corner. Next to it is Yuhikaku Publishers. Across the street from Yuhikaku is a new Thai
restaurant, **On The Menum** メナムの畔 ㉖, often crowded at
lunchtime, reflecting the recent fad for ethnic food. (*Open
11:30-14:30, 17:30-23:00. Closed on Sundays and national holidays.*)
A few buildings beyond Yuhikaku is **Yamagataya** 山形屋紙店
㉗, a paper shop selling high quality *washi* and stationery.

The local companies, shops, and residents have started a
new tradition; they organize an evening fair on the last Saturday of August every year, setting up stalls on both sides of the
street for each shop or company offering special bargain items.
Brass music played by the students of nearby junior high
schools adds to the festive mood. The idea of the festival is to
keep the community spirit alive in this area which has lost
many residents due to the proliferation of office buildings. The
summer fair has been quite successful and attracts many
people from near and far.

To return home, backtrack to the last traffic light and turn
left to reach the Jimbocho subway station.

Machi zentai ga toshokan mitai desu ne.
(The whole town is like a library.)

The Sumida River today   *courtesy Taito Ward*

Kagura dance at Shinagawa-jinja   *courtesy Shinagawa Ward*

Fukagawa Edo Museum   *courtesy Koto Ward*   ▶

Sarasa-zome stencil dyer   *photograph by Atsushi Matsushima*

Miniature
Edo kite
*photograph by
Susumu Matsushima*

Sogakudo
concert hall
courtesy Taito Ward

Jizo statue, Shinagawa   *courtesy Shinagawa Ward*

Guardian dog,
Nezu-jinja
*photograph by
Atsushi Matsushima*

Kokugikan
Sumo Arena
courtesy Sumida Ward

◀ Shinobazu Pond   *courtesy Taito Ward*

UENO

Walking time
Ueno–Toshogu–Shinobazu Pond: 1 hour
Toshogu–Kanei-ji–Shinobazu Pond: 1 hour 30 minutes
Ueno–Ameya Yokocho: 45 minutes

BACKGROUND Ueno was first renowned for its magnificent temple, Kanei-ji, erected by the shogunate in 1624 to protect the city of Edo from evil. Built on a hilltop, off-limits to commoners, the temple had large grounds beautifully laid out with a profusion of cherry trees. Unfortunately most of the temple buildings were lost during the civil war occasioned by the Meiji Restoration. The new Meiji government designated the hill and adjacent pond as a public park.

Today, Ueno has a strange charm resulting from the juxtaposition of old and new, common and precious, high and lowbrow. For example, on top of the hill stands the National Museum exhibiting some of the finest art in Japan and the world, while by Shinobazu Pond a small folk museum exhibits Tokyo's modest prewar lifestyles. Close to the great Shogun Ieyasu's mausoleum wild cormorants live and raise their young in Shinobazu Pond, surrounded by modern highrises.

GETTING THERE If you take the Ginza Line to Ueno, ascend the stairway in the middle of the platform. Pass through the ticket gate and turn right to take Exit 7. After exiting, turn left and walk straight to the traffic light ahead. If you arrive by the Hibiya Line, take the stairway at the end of the platform close to Naka-Okachimachi and turn left after the ticket gate

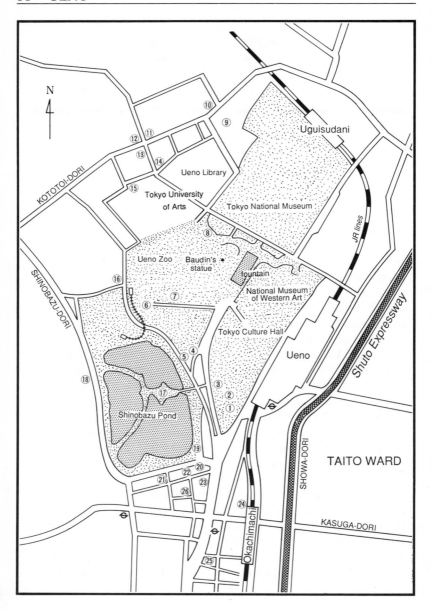

N

KOTOTOI-DORI

SHINOBAZU-DORI

⑩
⑨
⑫ ⑪
⑬ ⑭
⑮

Uguisudani

Ueno Library

Tokyo University
of Arts

Tokyo National Museum

⑧

Ueno Zoo   Baudin's
statue   fountain

⑯

National Museum
of Western Art

⑦
⑥

JR lines

⑤ ④

Tokyo Culture Hall

Ueno

③
②
①

⑱

⑰

Shinobazu Pond

Shuto Expressway

⑲

⑳
㉒
㉑   ㉓
㉖

SHOWA-DORI

TAITO WARD

㉔

KASUGA-DORI

Okachimachi

㉕

and take Exit 7 (or look for the arrow indicating transfer to the Ginza Line and follow it). If you take a JR train, get off at Ueno and descend the steps at the end of the platform closest to Okachimachi. Walk straight toward the Shinobazu Exit (しの ばず口) and turn right toward the traffic light mentioned above.

At the traffic light, cross the street and turn left. Ascend the large concrete stairway. At the top, look to the right to find a large bronze statue of **Saigo Takamori** 西郷隆盛像 ①, a leader in the Meiji Restoration. The statue, made by Koun Takamura in 1892, is one of the three most famous statues in Tokyo. Saigo Takamori was the chief of staff of an allied force made up of the Satsuma and Choshu clans from western Japan. They marched to Edo in 1868 to carry out an imperial order to overthrow the Tokugawa Shogunate. Katsu Awa, a vassal of the shogun, met Saigo at the Satsuma camp in Shinagawa and negotiated the bloodless surrender of Edo. The broad-minded Saigo agreed to save the city and its people from the destruction of war. Because of this humane decision, Saigo has long been remembered by the people of Tokyo as its savior.

Behind the statue on the left is a small compound with stone railings. In it is a **war memorial** 彰義隊記念碑 ② dedicated to a group of samurai who were killed here in the civil war of the same year.

Even after the bloodless surrender of Edo Castle on April 11, some proshogunate samurai continued to put up resistance, using this hill as their last stronghold. Their number swelled to a few thousand and defied the authority of the Satsuma-Choshu army, which was trying to establish control over the whole city in the name of the emperor. On May 15, the allied army attacked Ueno with guns and cannons. The resisters, fierce as they were, were overcome by the modern weapons of the imperial army, and the fight was over by the evening of the same day. The attack resulted in the loss of most of the magnificent buildings of Kanei-ji temple which stood on this hill.

Leave the small compound by the side exit near a bulletin board and bear right toward an attractive temple, **Kiyomizu Kannon** 清水観音 ③, a subsidiary temple of Kanei-ji dating from the seventeenth century. The architectural design is similar to Kiyomizu-dera in Kyoto, with its raised platform jutting over the side of the hill.

Kanei-ji was constructed with advice from a mysterious abbot called Tenkai. No one knew his background, but he was deeply trusted by Ieyasu and the next two shoguns. It was Tenkai who masterminded the construction of Nikko's Toshogu Mausoleum to serve as Ieyasu's permanent burial place. When the city of Edo was being built, Tenkai advised that a major temple should be constructed in the northeast of the city to prevent the invasion of evil spirits from that unlucky direction, just as Kyoto had Enryaku-ji on Mt. Hiei as well as Lake Biwa in its northeast direction. The city planners found the hill of Ueno and its neighboring pond to be in this unlucky direction and the hill was renamed Mt. Toei, meaning Hiei of the east. A splendid temple was built on the hilltop and was named Kanei-ji. As an added similarity to Kyoto, Kiyomizu Kannon was built in the same style as Kyoto's Kiyomizu-dera. This Kiyomizu Kannon, built in 1698, miraculously escaped the damage of the civil war and is a rare example of an Edo-period building in its original location in Tokyo.

The Kannon of this temple is supposed to respond to the prayers of worshipers having difficulty in bearing children. If successful, they return to pray for their child's continued health. Many types of dolls are brought to the temple as offerings, and are placed in the left-hand corner of the building. Every year on September 25, supposedly having completed their mission, these dolls are burned in a bonfire while priests chant sutras.

Descend the steps to a black wooden gate and turn right and walk a short distance along a gently curving boulevard lined with cherry trees. The path used to be the front approach to the main building of Kanei-ji. Edo commoners were allowed to enter about thus far for flower viewing. Of the many famous spots for cherry-blossom viewing in Edo, Ueno was the most elegant, and the women's kimono worn on this occasion would lead the year's fashion.

Soon, on the left of the boulevard, a dense tunnel of torii appears, indicating the entrance to an Inari shrine. Notice a pair of stone lions with enigmatic faces donated in 1753 by a local merchant. The tunnel of red gates descends to a shrine which is called **Hanazono Inari** 花園稲荷 ④. There is another shrine beyond, **Gojo Tenjin** 五条天神 ⑤. Through a gray torii you can glimpse the water of Shinobazu Pond.

Back at the boulevard, walk to the left. When you come to a totem pole, turn left and look for a stone torii opposite a group of colorful amusement facilities. The torii marks the entrance to **Toshogu** 東照宮 ⑥, a shrine dedicated to the first shogun, Ieyasu, in 1627. Including this stone gate, almost everything here is designated a national treasure or an important cultural asset. This shrine and its compound, too, survived the civil war and subsequent destruction in the 1923 earthquake and World War II air raids. As you walk into the shrine compound, you will be impressed by the rows of nearly two hundred stone lanterns which were donated by daimyo lords.

To the left of the approach is a peony garden which is open annually from January 1 to mid-February for winter peonies, and again from the end of April to mid-May for spring peonies. When the season comes, more than two thousand peony plants bloom, and the air is filled with their fragrance. April 17 is the date of the shrine's annual festival, and the compound bustles with many visitors.

Beyond a black metal fence on your right, a **five-story pagoda** 五重塔 ⑦ rises behind the trees. This beautiful 120-foot tower was built in 1639 as part of the facilities of Kanei-ji and is another precious legacy which has escaped many calamities. Formerly, there were six five-story pagodas in Edo, but only two remain today; the other is at Hommon-ji in western Tokyo.

To enter the main building, pay a small admission fee at the booth and then walk around the building to the entrance. This Toshogu shrine was built in 1651, fifteen years after the completion of Nikko Toshogu. The building, the sculptured walls, and the gate, along with other articles belonging to the shrine are national treasures. Upon entering, you will find yourself in the large Worship Hall where daimyo lords were seated. The painted lions by Kano Tanyu look menacingly at visitors.

Leaving the building, turn left and walk around the back to come to the splendid gate decorated with intricate carvings. The pair of magnificent long panels depicting dragons was reportedly carved by Hidari Jingoro, an artist of the Edo period. The wooden dragons are so lifelike that they were said to sneak out every night to Shinobazu Pond for a drink of water.

As you leave the shrine, notice a path to the right near the pagoda. It leads to a stone stairway descending through woods to a street by Shinobazu Pond. However, walk back to the main boulevard and turn left. A fountain ahead spouts water. Further in the distance lies the Tokyo National Museum, where the exquisite main building of Kanei-ji used to stand. A golden Buddha was enshrined in its interior and on both sides of the main building were rows of lesser temples. The sites of these subsidiary temples are now used for public facilities such as the Tokyo University of Arts, the Tokyo Metropolitan Museum of Arts, the National Science Museum, the Japan Academy, the National Museum of Western Arts, the Culture Hall, and the Japan Art Academy. In no other part of Tokyo are there so many high-level cultural facilities concentrated in one place.

When you come close to the fountain, look to your left. At the end of a dirt path stands the bronze bust of a Dutch military surgeon, Antonius F. Bauduin, who came to Japan to teach Western medical science, first in 1862 for three years, and again in 1869. He happened to learn about a government plan to build a large hospital on this hill which had been left desolate after the 1868 civil war. Admiring the rich nature and history of this area, he strongly urged the government officials to cancel the project and make the hill and its environs a public park—a novel idea to the Japanese of the time. Eventually, his suggestion was adopted and led to the opening of Ueno Park in 1876.

At the end of the rectangular pond which encloses the fountain, turn left. A lane meanders through woods toward a beige wooden building roofed with gray tiles. This is **Sogakudo** 奏楽堂 ⑧, built in 1890 and the oldest concert hall in Japan. As you walk up to it, glance to the right to see the massive gate of a daimyo residence in the distance. The gate was moved from its original site in Marunouchi to the current site for permanent preservation. The gate is the only structure remaining today which shows the style of the late Edo-period residences of the highest ranked lords who lived in Marunouchi.

The Sogakudo concert hall, and an organ of rare value installed there, have been preserved due to extensive citizens' movements. Originally built for the Tokyo School of Music, the predecessor of the present Tokyo University of Arts, this wooden hall was the cradle of Western music education, concerts, and opera in Japan. When it was designated to be taken down and replaced by a modern building in the early 1970s, many of the top-class musicians who had graduated from the school firmly opposed its demolition. Along with architectural historians and local citizens, they negotiated with the authorities for ten years, and finally succeeded in having the building preserved at local government expense. Now a property of Taito Ward, the beautifully refurbished hall is used for performances of classical music. *(It is open for public viewing on Tuesdays, Thursdays, and Sundays, 9:30–16:30, except December 29 to January 3. A small admission is charged.)* Inside, walk upstairs to enter the serenely peaceful and beautiful auditorium, often with taped organ music floating in the air.

Leaving Sogakudo, bear left to cross the intersection ahead toward a two-story brown brick building. A small pyramid-roofed gray building, also at this crossing, is the entrance to a station on the Keisei Line. Turn right along the side of the brick building. The next gray building is the Ueno Public Library with a large collection of books on Edo. Close to the fence, a monument is dedicated to Lafcadio Hearn, author and translator of Japanese folk tales, who taught at schools and universities in western Japan and Tokyo. Called Yakumo Koizumi in Japanese, he is perhaps the best known of all the foreign experts who came to Japan to guide the Japanese in Western knowledge.

Past the library, turn left and walk straight. Next to a school on the right is the current **Kanei-ji** 寛永寺⑨, which stands on the site of one of its former subsidiary temples. Since the original Kanei-ji was lost in the civil war of 1868, this building was moved in 1877 from Kita-in, Kawagoe, a large temple once administered by Abbot Tenkai, the original founder of Kanei-ji.

Leaving Kanei-ji, turn right, and at a T-junction cross over to **Jomyo-in temple** 浄名院⑩, situated on slightly lower ground on the other side of the street. The temple is famous for the rows of 14,000 numbered statues of Jizo which fill its garden. When the temple was founded in 1850, the abbot of the temple made a vow to set up one thousand Jizo. The vow was fulfilled in 1879, and the abbot then made another vow to set up 84,000 statues. This goal has been taken over by the succeeding abbots. It is an astonishing sight to see row upon row of stone figures, some decayed by age, standing in orderly silence.

If you wish to finish the tour here, you can reach Uguisudani Station on the JR Yamanote and Keihin Tohoku lines in about five minutes. Turn left at the temple's exit and cross over to the other side of the street so that you walk along the right side of the bridge over the railroads ahead. Descend the stairway at the end of the bridge and walk straight to the next traffic light, where you should turn right to come to the station. Trains bound for Tokyo leave from either track 3 or 4.

To continue, however, turn right. You have to endure the heavy traffic for a few minutes until you come to the third traffic light. On the corner of this crossing stands the traditional building of a former liquor shop, **Yoshidaya** 吉田屋⑪. It is another example of successful landmark preservation due to the efforts of concerned citizens. With a long stretch of front eaves and pairs of latticed shutters, the two-story wooden building was built in 1910 and shows the representative style of a late Meiji-era shop in Tokyo. This building too was destined to be demolished. The same groups of local preservationists who worked for the Sogakudo raised their voices, and won the cooperation of the local government. Now, as an annex to the Shitamachi Museum by Shinobazu Pond, it is open to public viewing free of charge.

In this neighborhood are some good places for a break. At the intersection are **Kayaba coffee shop** カヤバコーヒー ⑫ on the right as you leave the Yoshidaya building, and **Waka Sushi** 和花鮨 across the street from it. *(Closed on Mondays.)* A few buildings away from the sushi restaurant along a small lane forking out from the main street is a good French restaurant, **Pepe Le Moko** ペペルモコ ⑬. A large room upstairs may be reserved for a group of up to two dozen. Full-course menus are available at reasonable prices. *(Open 11:30–14:30 and 17:00-22:00. Closed on Wednesdays. Tel: 3823-7387.)* Passing the French restaurant, you will find **Torindo** 桃林堂 ⑭, a Japanese sweet shop, on the left of the next small intersection. Originally from Osaka, the shop sells candied vegetables and fruits. Cross the intersection here and turn right to walk along the metal guard rails to the next traffic light.

A temple on the left of this crossing is **Gokoku-in** 護国院 ⑮, which is dedicated to Daikoku, one of the seven lucky gods in the Yanaka area. The design of a mallet, usually associated with this god, is used on the offering box and curtains. The main building dates from 1722. The third day of every month is a special day for prayers at this temple.

Leaving Gokoku-in, turn left around the exterior wall of the temple and walk along the compound of a large, modern high school. The road, which descends slowly along the west side of the hill of Ueno, has been known as Shimizu-zaka since the eighteenth century. As you walk, look ahead for a distant view of the five-story pagoda, which is visible above the woods.

Continuing downhill, turn left at a T-junction with traffic lights. You are heading for Shinobazu Pond. A relatively large six-story building on the way is **Suigetsu Hotel** 水月ホテル⑯, which has a dining room facing the road for walk-in guests. Proceeding along the main road, you will go under the overhead monorail for visitors to the zoo. A stone torii on the left of the road marks the bottom of the stone stairway descending from Toshogu. Another torii a little further beyond is the side exit from Gojo Tenjin shrine.

At the next traffic light, a large red torii can be seen on the right-hand side of the road; walk through it to a shrine on an island at the center of the pond. It is dedicated to **Benten** 辯才 天 ⑰, the goddess of fortune and music, who is associated with water and serpents. Therefore, the days of the serpent are the shrine's fair days. The summer festival from mid-July until early August is a lively affair with many stalls in and around the shrine. The shrine building is relatively new; with its octagonal roof-line rising above reeds and lotuses in the pond, it looks better from a distance. The paintings of a dragon on the ceiling, and spring and autumn flowers on the panels flanking the altar are works of Kibo Kodama, a famous artist of Japanese painting, and his students. A short detour from here will take you to a small museum related to an even more famous leader in traditional painting, Taikan Yokoyama.

*   *   *

SUGGESTED DETOUR   Walk along the right side of the shrine and then turn to the right at the boathouse. The right-hand section of the pond is part of the zoo and is home to wild birds. The large black ones are *kawau* (a kind of cormorant), which nest and raise their young in this pond. The colony of wild cormorants at Ueno receives much attention from ornithologists worldwide. At the main street, take the crossing to your left and turn left to come to the entrance of the **Yokoyama Tai-kan Memorial House** 横山大観記念館 ⑱, where the famous painter lived the last fifty years of his life. *(Open 10:00-16:00,*

Thursday through Sunday. Closed in August, and mid-December through mid-January. A small admission is charged.)

Taikan Yokoyama was one of the greatest artists of modern Japanese painting. As the most enthusiastic follower of Tenshin Okakura (see pages 105–106), Taikan devoted his early life to putting Tenshin's theory of new traditionalism into practice in his own paintings. The two artists attempted to revitalize traditional Japanese painting, which had become overstructured since the mid-Edo period. They tried, for example, not to use the fine linear brushwork which was, and still is, regarded as the leading characteristic of Japanese painting.

*   *   *

Retrace your steps to the red torii of the Benten shrine and turn right to your next destination, the Shitamachi Museum, on the other side of the pond. This section of the pond is covered with lotus leaves in spring and summer. The deep-pink lotus flowers are often used to symbolize the pond. Large flocks of migratory birds come from Siberia to spend the winter, and dragonflies flit about in the summer. The rich natural setting of the pond is appreciated by residents and visitors alike, but has been threatened a number of times in the past—with plans to fill it in to build a baseball field, to turn it into rice paddies during the last war, or as recently as in the late 1980s, to build a large car park underneath the pond. Each time, people who love the pond got together to stop the construction.

A little off to the left of the pond stands a relatively small black-and-white building with a few colorful banners in front. This is the **Shitamachi Museum** 下町風俗資料館 ⑲, opened in 1980 to preserve and exhibit various aspects of the common people's life in prewar Tokyo. The main items on permanent display are a merchant house and a tenement house. These are life-size reproductions of Shitamachi housing in the early twentieth century, a time when the towns of Shitamachi retained much of the Edo style with relatively little influence from Meiji industrialization. Many people from that time are still alive to contribute their memories and articles to the resources of the museum. The ingenious layout of furniture and utensils makes the visitor feel as if the residents of the houses could return any minute. You may touch the display and step into the rooms if you take off your shoes. The second floor is for videotaped displays and exhibitions of various tools and toys which were commonly used in prewar days. Demonstrations of making simple crafts are often organized and visitors are encouraged to participate. *(Open 9:30-16:30, Tuesdays through Sundays. Closed December 29-January 3. An English brochure is available.)*

As you come out of the museum, notice Kentucky Fried Chicken on the other side of the street to the left. To its right is a small comb shop, **Jusanya** 十三屋 ⑳, in business since 1736. This shop is like a miniature comb museum exhibiting many kinds of combs and tiny figurines made of boxwood, the material for combs. Some of these old combs could never be reproduced nowadays because the skills needed to make them have died out. High quality boxwood is becoming rarer and rarer too, and the precious wood must be left for as long as ten years before it is ready to be cut and made into combs. After sixty stages, each requiring meticulous care, one comb is ready for sale.

Leaving the comb shop, turn left and left again at the next traffic light. Around the corner to the right of the next crossing is a small silk-braid shop, **Domyo** 道明 ㉑. The narrow braids are used to tighten *obi* (kimono sashes). Maintaining the traditions of braid making as well as traditional business style, the shop displays the subtly colored products in lacquered trays placed on a tatami-matted floor. In the small display window, string ties for men and belts for Western-style dresses are exhibited as part of the attempts of the shop's eighth-generation owner to adjust ancient expertise to modern needs.

From Domyo, turn left and cross the street to visit an excellent prewar-style furniture shop, **Kyoya** 京屋 ㉒, in the third building on the left from the crossing. It is another shop making dedicated efforts to preserve old traditions, in this case, fine woodwork called Edo *sashimono*. Carefully selected and pre-pared pieces of wood are assembled by matching joints to make cabinets, chests of drawers, or boxes. *(Open 10:00-18:00. Closed on Sundays.)*

Continuing straight from Kyoya, walk toward the red-and-white heart logo of the Dai-Ichi Kangyo Bank, and you will come to the main street. To the right is **Suzumoto** 鈴本演芸館 ㉓, a theater specializing in *rakugo* and other narrative arts. It is now housed in a modern building and banners mark its entrance. At this spot, you can catch the red double-decker, London-style bus for Asakusa. Between Suzumoto and the bank, **Shuetsu** 酒悦 has sold various Japanese pickles since the Edo period.

The main street here is Chuo-dori extending from Nihombashi. Cross it toward a large apparel shop called ABAB and turn left along its right-hand side. As you walk toward the elevated railway ahead of you, you will see a bustling market area called **Ameya Yokocho** アメヤ横町 ㉔, which is in the space beneath the railway and along the adjacent streets. These shops are survivors of the confused economy right after World War II when illegal food and foreign goods were sold on the black market. The area still bustles with nearly four hundred cramped shops dealing in fish, cosmetics, imported apparel, sundries, and even jewels. In no other place in Japan can you find salmon and cod roe in juxtaposition with diamonds and emeralds. Throughout the year this place is like one constant festival, and business thrives. It is a fascinating area to explore and enjoy shopping or browsing for a while.

Back at Chuo-dori, turn left to the entrance of Hirokoji Station on the Ginza Line. The station is connected to the basement of Matsuzakaya Department Store. Incidentally, this area is generally acknowledged as the birthplace of *tonkatsu* (Japanese pork cutlets) and so there are many such restaurants around here. The one which claims the honor of originating the recipe is **Ponta** ぽん多 ㉕. The restaurant is straight ahead, past a pedestrian bridge, to the left of the traffic light. On the corner is Mitsubishi Trust Bank. Look for a short blue *noren* next to a coffee shop. Ponta is a neat, typical Shitamachi restaurant. Almost an inch thick, the piping hot *tonkatsu* is juicy and tender. Rice and *akadashi* (bean soup) must be ordered separately. *(Open 11:00–14:00, 16:30–20:00. Closed on Mondays.)*

Another *tonkatsu* restaurant which competes in popularity with Ponta is **Futaba** 双葉 ㉖. Backtrack to the subway entrance, cross Chuo-dori and turn right. Turn left at the corner of JTB. Futaba is on the right-hand corner of the next small crossing. Try *tonkatsu teishoku*. *(Open most days, 11:00–15:00, 17:00–20:30.)* In case Futaba is closed, **Musashino** 武蔵野 near the same crossing is also good and less expensive. To return, walk back to the subway station, or go to Ueno Station.

Ueno ni wa himitsu no poketto ga takusan arimasu.
(Ueno has many secret pockets.)

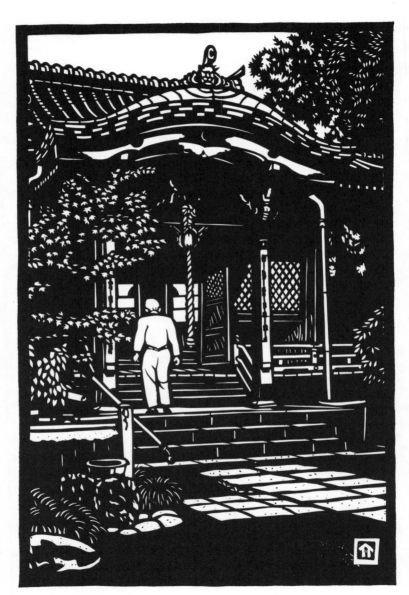

6
YANAKA

Walking time
North Yanaka: 1 hour
South Yanaka: 45 minutes

BACKGROUND   Yanaka is an old temple town which dates back to the time when the Tokugawa Shogunate placed clusters of temples around Edo's periphery so that the temple buildings could be used as forts to protect the inner city from military invasion. Fortunately, the 260 years of Tokugawa rule passed peacefully, and the temples thrived under shogunate patronage. The temples also had the strong support of the townspeople, who seemed to visit the temples more for reasons of fashion than out of religious fervor. Because of rapid postwar urbanization, most of the temple towns have lost their one-time popularity and prestige. Yanaka is an exception, and you will see on this tour a concentration of temples which have escaped destruction from both man-made and natural disasters.

Yanaka and its environs were also famous for their scenic woodlands and clear streams. During the Meiji era, and for some time afterward, many artists and literati lived in this part of Tokyo and engaged in various cultural activities. A small but extremely pretty garden, formerly belonging to one such artist, is the highlight of this course. The garden is part of the Asakura Sculpture Museum which itself looks like a gigantic sculpture and houses the work of one of Japan's foremost Western-style sculptors.

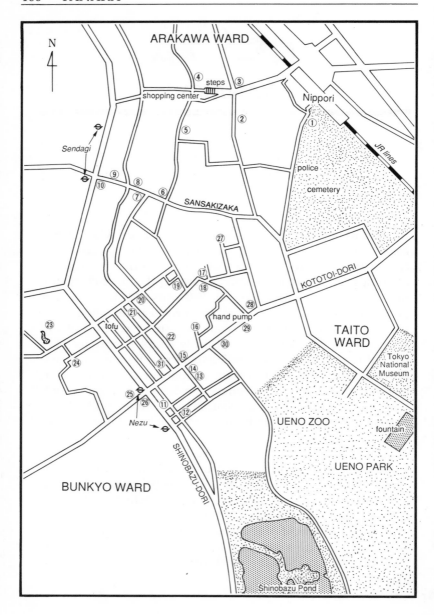

NORTH YANAKA

GETTING THERE   Take the JR Yamanote Line or Keihin
Tohoku Line to Nippori Station. When you get off the train,
walk to the end of the platform closest to Nishi Nippori and
ascend the stairway. After passing through the ticket-gate, turn
left. Instead of taking the large road leading away from the exit,
walk up the steps built between stone walls and pay phones to
the left. At its top is the Yanaka cemetery. A stone-paved path
under an arch of cherry trees winds past gravestones on both
sides, bending to the left and joining a concrete-paved road.

A Japanese grave is nowadays usually used for one entire
family. On the front of the gravestone is engraved the family
name and on the sides are the names of the family members
whose bones and ashes are buried beneath. The wooden sticks
behind the gravestone are called *sotoba* from the Sanskrit
"stupa," and are offered by the bereaved family on the occasion of anniversary services for the dead. The writing on the
sticks differs according to the Buddhist sect, but usually shows
the posthumous name of the person to whom the sticks are
dedicated.

When you come to the concrete road, you will see the
temple **Tenno-ji** 天王寺 ① on your left. As you walk into the
cleanly swept temple compound, you will notice a beautiful
bronze Buddha seated in meditation on a high pedestal; cast in
1690, it is one of the hidden treasures of the area. During the
Edo period, the temple compound was about ten times its present size. Now, with so few people around, it is hard to imagine
its former prosperity, but the extensive graveyard which used
to be part of the temple's property gives an idea of its former
prestige.

Tenno-ji, which was founded in the fifteenth century,
thrived in the eighteenth century as one of the three Edo
temples authorized to hold lotteries. On the day of a lottery
drawing, the temple compound was full of people dreaming of

winning a fortune. An Edo-period public lottery used a big wooden box which contained numbered wooden tablets corresponding to subscription tickets sold in advance. The box was placed in front of the temple, and as a sutra was chanted, an officer of the lottery drove a long gimlet into the box, pulling out the lucky tablets one at a time. It is said that each win called caused a great stir and threw the crowd into feverish excitement. Because year after year the lottery boom grew wilder and more out of control, lotteries were eventually banned in the middle of the nineteenth century.

Close to the roofed gate of the temple is a small but quite impressive building dedicated to Bishamon, one of the seven lucky gods in the Yanaka area. The building itself was erected in 1961, using the remains of the burnt-down pagoda described below. Its doors are open during the first three days of January when you can see an old wooden statue of Bishamon dating from the mid-Heian period. The Yanaka course of the lucky god walks is the oldest of numerous similar tours in this city and attracts people from near and far. (The starting point is the Benten shrine at Shinobazu Pond, where you can buy a woodblock print of the seven gods on which the inscriptions and stamps of each temple you visit are placed.)

Just outside the current compound, there was once a beautiful five-story pagoda; much celebrated for its masterly workmanship, the pagoda and the carpenter who built it were immortalized in a short story written by Rohan Koda, a Meiji-era writer. Its ingenious structure enabled it to withstand many earthquakes, but in 1957 a fire started by a love suicide reduced it to ashes. Only the geometrically arranged foundation stones remain today.

Leaving the temple, follow the main road of the cemetery. In the spring, this road becomes a long tunnel of cherry blossoms and is crowded with merrymakers. Though a peaceful burial place now, two hundred years ago this area was by no means quiet, with its rows of teahouses serving refreshments to Tenno-ji visitors. Little by little these shops also began to accommodate the sensual desires which attracted many male customers, including priests from neighboring temples. Osen, a pretty young woman who worked at one of the teahouses, became particularly famous when the ukiyo-e artist Harunobu depicted her in numerous prints. The popularity created by the fast sale of these prints gave her many admirers. Apparently, she was smart enough not to be carried away by her feverish popularity, and retiring from the flowery service, she married a somber low-class samurai and had a long life.

When you come to a police box on the left of the road, glance at the bamboo-fenced site of the pagoda a little off to the left. Local witnesses of the fire still remember the sight of the blazing pagoda, more than thirty years ago, and are looking for a way to rebuild it. Turn right at this crossing and go to the end of the road, where you turn right again. Soon, you will come to a three-story black concrete building with some statues in front. This is the **Asakura Sculpture Museum** 朝倉彫塑館 ②, originally the home and studio of Fumio Asakura, a master of Western-style sculpture, which has recently been donated to Taito Ward. It has a gem of a garden inside. *(Open 9:30-16:30. Closed on Mondays and Fridays, or the following day when either of these weekdays falls on a national holiday, as well as the government holidays from December 29 to January 3. A small admission is charged. Tel: 3821-4549.)*

As you enter the atelier, you will see a huge statue of a man in a cap and gown. This is Shigenobu Okuma, a famous statesman of the late nineteenth and early twentieth centuries, who was the founder of Waseda University. Among the other numerous statues and busts, there is one of an unusually tall man, Shimpei Goto, another Meiji-era statesman and Mayor of Tokyo. An extremely prolific artist, Asakura made over four-hundred statues during his lifetime. He was a great cat lover and his lovely lifelike statuettes of these little animals can be seen on the second floor.

The private area adjacent to the atelier and the study is designed to look out on a rectangular pond. The pond was designed as a water garden in contrast to the better known dry rock garden. The water gushes out from under the atelier, lapping the different-shaped stones. These stones represent five important Confucian virtues: benevolence, righteousness, propriety, wisdom, and sincerity. The layout of the stones has been designed as a reminder against the abuse of these virtues. For instance, the meek stone of benevolence has been worn smooth by the constant lapping of the water. The proud stone of righteousness is hushed in silence by a covering of ferns. The stable stone of propriety humbly supports the bridge, and the stone of wisdom hides its intellectual depth in thick foliage. The top of the last stone, sincerity, can barely be seen above the water. The whole design, therefore, represents an ethical ideal.

Walk around the pond and observe the tea room which is on the opposite side. Turning left at the first corner of the corridor, note particularly the simple beauty of the private entrance. Follow the arrows to tour the building.

Leaving the museum, turn right. The road crosses a large street leading from Nippori Station to the right. Cross over to a temple, **Kyo-o-ji** 経王寺 ③. The heavy wooden doors of the temple's front gate retain bullet holes from the civil war in 1868 when the last and fiercest group of the shogun's supporters fought against the coalition army of the Satsuma and Choshu clans. Turn around to walk away from the JR station. Descend the stairway. Just before the shopping street ahead, turn right to visit a charming basket shop, **Buseki Flower Basket Shop** 武関花篭細工 ④, with many pots of small bonsai on shelves in front and indoors.

To visitors from concrete-bound central Tokyo, this shop is a virtual haven, with its lovely baskets hung on the walls and placed on shelves. Expensive items are made from smoked bamboo; the rich, glossy color comes from years of being smoked over a fire pit in a thatched farm house. This bamboo, part of the material used in thatching roofs, is sold to be crafted into various things. As modern building material and industrial products now permeate even the remotest rural areas, good quality smoked bamboo is becoming hard to find. *(Open 9:00-18:00.)*

Leaving the basket shop, go back to the entrance of the shopping center to the right. A quick detour to the right will provide a good chance to look around the shops. On each lamppost are attached two square glass panels depicting famous landscapes in Yanaka, these are works by Ryosuke Ishida, a celebrated paper-cut artist. Your direction, however, is straight on. Soon, you will come to a **small park** ⑤ on the left. The park is in memory of Tenshin Okakura and the Japan Arts Institute (Nihon Bijutsuin) 岡倉天心記念公園 which he founded in 1898. A hexagonal shrine houses a golden bust of Okakura in the institute's Nara-period uniform. The bust is the work of Denchu Hiragushi, a top contemporary sculptor whose masterpiece is a carved Kabuki lion-dancer on exhibit at the National Theater.

Tenshin Okakura, author of *The Book of Tea,* was a passionate leader and theorist of modern Japanese painting in the early Meiji era. He was born in Yokohama, the son of a samurai in the export business. Well-versed in both Chinese classics and English, he met Ernest F. Fenollosa, who came to Japan in 1876 to teach at what is now the University of Tokyo. Okakura was a student at that time, and his good knowledge of English was extremely helpful to Fenollosa. Okakura cultivated a deep knowledge of traditional fine arts through his many years of association with Fenollosa. In the midst of the trend towards Westernization, Okakura and Fenollosa advocated the traditional arts, particularly Japanese painting, and worked hard to have their ideas adopted by the Tokyo Fine Arts School, the predecessor of the current Tokyo University of Arts. In 1898 Okakura founded the Japan Fine Arts Institute which was located on this site.

Okakura's passionate discussions and stimulating suggestions led to the creation of an entirely new style of Japanese painting. One idea which was pursued by his devoted followers, despite public scorn and harsh criticism, was the rejection of line drawing. The artists who were inspired by Okakura include such famous names in contemporary Japanese painting as Taikan Yokoyama, Shunso Hishida, and Kanzan Shimomura.

Leaving the park, turn left and walk straight on until you come to a crossing with a traffic light. You will pass a brick wall on the right which surrounds a big temple, the entrance of which is a few doors away from the corner. This temple, **Daien-ji** 大円寺 ⑥, is famous for two memorial stones dedicated to Harunobu, the ukiyo-e artist, and his model, the beautiful Osen, mentioned earlier. These stones are on the right of the path from the gate, on either side of a Kannon statue. The taller stone is Harunobu's, and the smaller, Osen's. On October 14 and 15 every year, a Chrysanthemum Festival is held in the temple compound. More than three-thousand pots of the flower are displayed, many of them for sale, and a variety of stalls sell cotton candy, *yakisoba*, and toys. In the evening, a fantastic performance of traditional dance is given by bonfire light.

The street in front of Daien-ji is called Sansakizaka. You may go left here to explore some prewar wooden buildings and walk eventually into Ueno Park. For now however, cross the road and turn right. On the corner of the next small crossing is **Rampo** 乱歩 for coffee and snacks. Beyond it is a charming paper shop, **Isetatsu** いせ辰 ⑦, selling traditional Japanese paper products. High up on the wall of the building are Edo-style shop signs, and a red-carpeted bench adds to the atmosphere. Inside, the shop is filled with papier-mâché animals, pretty chest of drawers covered with printed paper, and other small items which make wonderful gifts. Founded in 1858, the shop specializes in the production and sale of colorfully printed Japanese paper called *chiyogami*. The designs have evolved from decorations on kimono and armor used by court nobility and samurai. Printed on paper, the beautiful designs were brought within reach of the common people and were very popular during the Edo period. The dainty but rigid style of armor decorations became more sophisticated in the eighteenth and nineteenth centuries, adopting the free and easy style of the Edo townspeople. The best designs were created at this time and have been unrivaled ever since.

As you go left from Isetatsu, look for two good restaurants on the other side of the street, close to the next traffic light. **Noike** 乃池 ⑧ serves excellent sushi at reasonable prices. Its speciality is *anago-zushi* (sushi with delicately cooked conger), available also for takeout. *(Open 11:30-14:00 and 16:30-21:00. Closed on Tuesdays.)* Next to it is **Oshimaya** 大島屋 noodle restaurant, where you might enjoy *jigoku* (hell) or *gokuraku* (paradise) noodles, served with a sesame-flavored sauce. The hell dish is served hot and the paradise cold. Turn right here and take the second small lane to the left and you will find **Kana Kana** かなかな, a neat handicrafts shop. Further along the main thoroughfare on the right is **Kikumi Senbei** 菊見煎餅 ⑨, selling hand-made rice crackers. Straight ahead is Sendagi Station on the Chiyoda Line. If you would like a rest, on this side of the intersection is another coffee shop, **Sendagi Kurabu** 千駄木倶楽部 ⑩.

SOUTH YANAKA

If you are continuing your walk, buy the least expensive ticket from the machine and take the train to the next stop, Nezu, from track 1. Get on a car at the front of the train and ascend the steps to Exit 2. The large road in front of the exit is the Shinobazu-dori, named after Shinobazu Pond. Cross the road and walk straight on. At the next crossing, turn left and take the second small lane to the right. On this corner, a large sign advertises Kondo Gallery, your next destination. Before turning right, look ahead to the left at a very attractive old-fashioned three-story building, **Hantei** はん亭 ⑪, a *kushiage* (skewered deep-fried meat and vegetables) restaurant. *(Open 17:00-20:00. Closed on Mondays.)* The left-hand section of the building houses a small coffee shop which also serves simple lunches, such as curry with rice or *soboro bentō* (ground chicken over rice in a box) with coffee or tea. *(Open 11:30-14:00 and 18:00-22:00 on Tuesday through Saturday, and 12:00-18:00 on Sundays and holidays.)*

Kondo コンドー ⑫ , is a small gallery in a tile-covered building on the right. Exhibitions are usually of woodblock prints, sketches, and crafts, selected to reflect the atmosphere of the neighborhood. In the right-hand corner of the gallery, beautiful kimono materials and small, unusual items are displayed for sale. *(Open 11:00-18:00. Closed on Mondays.)*

From the gallery, turn right and then left at the next crossroads. This street is lined with small shops, including **Bika** 美華 ⑬ , a Chinese restaurant in a modern tiled building on the right. Their lunches are delicious. *(Closed on Tuesdays.)* Five buildings beyond is an excellent *kaiseki* caterer, **Uozen** 魚善 ⑭ , which has two small rooms upstairs available for lunch and dinner upon reservation. Their traditional cuisine definitely deserves a try. *(For reservation, call 3821-4351. Open 12:00-22:00. Closed on Thursdays.)* Right next to it is a casual bar-style restaurant and coffee shop, **Flip-Flap**. At lunchtime, hamburgers and spaghetti are served at reasonble prices. *(Open 9:00-22:00. Usually closed on Sundays. To confirm, call 3828-7007.)* Both Bika and Flip-Flap are crowded around noon, so it's better to go early or late.

When you come to the next major intersection, cross the road at the nearby traffic light toward a *sembei* shop, **Daikoku-ya** 大黒屋 ⑮ , where you sometimes see men pressing and turning rice cakes on a charcoal fire—the secret for making crisp, savory rice crackers. Turn right and walk past a dozen or so buildings before approaching several large trees and a pair of stone lanterns marking the entrance to a temple, **Gyokurin-ji** 玉林寺 ⑯ , on the left. Enter through its front gate, but instead of walking up to the main building, take a small cement path to the right. Bearing to the left along the temple's side wall, walk up some steps on the right. At the bottom of this stairway is a wonderful old-fashioned hand pump, still in use by neighbors for washing or watering plants. A Shitamachi community used to be formed around a well like this where women from the neighborhood gathered to wash and draw water for household use. Lively conversation naturally developed and hence, an informal discussion meeting is still referred to as *idobata kaigi*, meaning "wellside meeting."

After the steps, the lane bends to the left and then right. At a T-junction, go left to come to a fork in the road. You have two alternatives here: the left includes, among other things, the Daimyo Clock Museum and Nezu-jinja, and the right will take you to some more temples and interesting shops.

ALTERNATIVE ONE   To the left are some interesting temples. The one on the right is the quiet, pretty **Renge-ji** 蓮華寺 ⑰, with its red wooden gate of bold but simple design, dating back to the Edo period. The garden is well-tended, and the carvings on the transoms over the staircase are very attractive. This temple is well known for exorcising worms believed to be responsible for children's tempers and insomnia.

The temple across the road, **Enju-ji** 延寿寺 ⑱, is also known for its healing powers: in this case, leg troubles. On the tenth of every month, big red lanterns are put up on both sides of the black gate, indicating the prayer day for healing, and the temple is crowded with many worshipers. Founded in the mid-seventeenth century, the temple is related to St. Nikka of the Nichiren sect of Buddhism, who was famous for his strong legs. It is said that he carried two huge 12-foot-high statues 150 miles from the coast to the top of Mt. Minobu all by himself. The statues are still at the head temple of the sect. In the mid-eighteenth century a statue of St. Nikka, which had originally been housed at the main temple, was moved here and subsequently attracted numerous worshipers. Many straw sandals are hung around the beams of the prayer hall. These were donated in appreciation of cures. Healing temples such as these two were extremely popular among the people in Edo and prewar Tokyo, and there were a great number of them, each with a specialty developed from a legend or an incident related to the cure.

In Edo, according to a law laid down by the Tokugawa Shogunate, all commoners had to be registered at a temple of an authorized sect. Temples themselves were organized in hierarchical order and were supposed to educate the people in their teachings. In practice, commoners cared little about the authenticity of the creed; being pragmatic, not to mention whimsical, they would go to any temple which would answer their prayers, and their most serious concern was health. According to a handbook on people's wishes, published in 1814, recovery from illness tops all the others.

From Enju-ji, turn left and then left again. Another street will soon join from the right. A thickly wooded compound on the right, behind a convex mirror for motorists, is the **Daimyo Clock Museum** 大名時計博物館 ⑲ which houses a private collection of old clocks. To visit, turn right and then left around the wall. An old wooden gate marks the entrance; the display room is in the gray stucco building to the left, too modest to house the rare collection. If it is closed, call *gomen kudasai!* (Hello! Is anyone there?) at the house to your right. *(Open 10:00–16:00. Closed on Mondays, the day after a national holiday, or from July 1 through September 30, and December 25 through January 15. A small fee is charged.)* Japanese clocks were a unique invention of the Edo period, adopting a time-keeping method seen nowhere else at the time. One hour was not a fixed period of time—one hour during the day was not the same as one hour during the night, nor was one summer hour the same as one winter hour. This was because time keeping was geared to sunrise and sunset, which naturally differed according to the season.

Primitive Japanese clocks had just one balance bar and needed to be adjusted manually twice a day by moving the weight on the balance. This meant that each clock had to be attended by someone who knew how to reset it. In addition to the huge expense of the devices themselves, which are of gorgeous craftmanship, the high operating costs were such that only daimyo and extremely wealthy merchants could afford them. This type of clock is therefore called a daimyo clock. Clocks later had two balance bars for both the daytime and the nighttime which could be switched automatically, but they still needed to be adjusted bi-monthly in order to catch up with seasonal changes. The twelve hours in the Japanese timekeeping system were given the names of the twelve animals in the Chinese zodiac. Twelve o'clock noon was the hour of the horse, and twelve o'clock midnight was the hour of the rat.

There was also a non-mechanical invention which was called a *kōdokei,* or incense clock. By burning incense and measuring the progress of the smoke, the approximate time of day could be told. As these devices could only be purchased by the very rich, there were nine temples in the city authorized by the shogunate to ring time bells twelve times a day, or sometimes just twice a day to indicate sunrise and sunset. There is a famous haiku poem, which is related to this practice:

> Clouds of cherry blossoms
> Is this bell I hear from Ueno
> Or from Asakusa?

Leaving the museum, turn left and take the first left, which is a downhill street leading to an intersection with a traffic light straight ahead. At the first crossroads before that is **Sawano-ya inn** 澤の屋 ⑳, to your left. The inn is popular among non-Japanese visitors who like to try Japanese *ofuro* (bath) and futon bedding on tatami. It is a modest, family-run establishment, but the hospitality is excellent and the charges very reasonable. *(For details and reservations, call 3822-2251.)* Past Sawano-ya, you can take the first left for a short detour to see some old houses and interesting stone statues.

* * *

SUGGESTED DETOUR   Turn left at the first small crossing after Sawano-ya. A few buildings away on the right is the old wooden building of a dyer, **Choji-ya** 染物丁字屋 ㉑ . Further on, a small lane joins from the left, and a few houses and a car park beyond it, on the left, is a Zen temple, **Rinko-ji** 臨江寺 ㉒ . Inside a roofed gate at the end of a stone path to the left, a group of small stone bas-reliefs have been placed around a smooth granite stone. All the stones are memorials, not graves, given to pray for the repose of the souls of the dead. The arch-shaped contour is supposed to represent a boat which takes the dead across a river to the afterworld and is characteristic of this kind of Edo-period bas-relief. The central figure is either a Kannon, if it has a crown on its head and a lotus stalk in hand, or a Jizo, if it has a bare head and a ball in hand. The characters inscribed on the stones represent the posthumous name of the person to whom the statue is dedicated, usually written on the right, on the other side is the year of dedication. Due to weathering, the names are not easy to read. The decipherable ones, particularly those of children, reveal poetic combinations of kanji characters conveying the deep love of the bereaved family. For instance, one on the right in the far back, donated in 1775, reads, "Moonlit garden, illusory light, little girl." Another one reads, "Illusion, clear and bright gem, little boy." Bas-reliefs of this type started in the Edo period. The oldest one here was donated in 1673, most of the others are from the eighteenth century. Under the shogunate's strict religious policy, only daimyo and samurai were allowed to have gravestones, and these were erected in a specific style demonstrating their dignity and prestige. Commoners were allowed only a pebble to mark their graves. In 1657, however, a fire broke out which reduced most of the city to ashes and took a heavy toll of 107,000 lives. Shortly afterwards, bas-relief stones like the ones here began to appear. It soon became popular among commoners to dedicate small bas-reliefs to the dead, and since these were memorials and not gravestones, it was a way of getting around the shogunate's ban. The deep grief behind these bas-reliefs continues to touch people's hearts nowadays, and one often sees flowers or other offerings placed beside them.

*   *   *

After Rinko-ji, return to the road from Sawano-ya. Continue straight on past a good tofu shop, **Echigo-ya** 越後屋, on the left of the road. Cross the main road, Shinobazu-dori, toward a fruit shop on the other side. Keep straight on until you see the torii of **Nezu-jinja** 根津神社 ㉓ ahead. In the spacious compound, the sharp geometric pattern of stone paths contrasts with the luxuriantly crafted and colored gates and main building, dating from 1706. These were donated by the fifth shogun to pay homage to his adopted son's tutelary shrine. A few years later, this son became the sixth shogun. The hillside on the left is planted with many azaleas, which bloom in late April and early May, providing an occasion for a big festival, Tsutsuji Matsuri (April 14 to May 5). On the hilltop, tunnels of red torii lead to a subsidiary shrine which is dedicated to Inari. During the festival period, the main building opens to visitors. The purpose is to show the paintings of thirty-six classical poets hung along transoms inside. The building opens only for half an hour at 10:00, 12:00, 14:00, and 16:00 each day. When there are too many visitors, the number is restricted. Buy a ticket from a priest in a nearby tent and proceed to the main building. You need to be purified by another priest before entering the altar area, which is a rare experience for most non-Japanese. *(For more details, call 3822-0753.)*

Leaving the shrine from the front torii, retrace your steps a short distance and take the first right. At a T-junction, **Shanhairo**上海楼 ㉔, a large inn, stands on the other side of the road to the left. Beyond it is a surprise—a church. Painted in pale blue and capped with a brown pinnacle, the charming wooden building blends in nicely with the Shitamachi community. Straight ahead is a crossing with the Shinobazu-dori. Turning right, you will come to Nezu Station on the Chiyoda Line, on the right of a major intersection.

If you turn right past the subway entrance, there is a cozy coffee shop, **Bon** ボン ㉕, with a black-and-yellow shop sign, close to a bright-red mail box. Ascend the stairway to the second floor. If you are hungry and care for spaghetti, **Spiga** スピ

ガ ㉖ is recommended. It is on the other side of the road from Bon, with a brick facade. A great variety of tasty spaghetti and salad are offered, utilizing many Japanese ingredients. *(Open 11:30-15:00 and 17:00-20:45. Closed on Thursdays.)*

ALTERNATIVE TWO   Your direction is to the right, passing the front of a tiny shop at a triangular crossing. The two temples described in Alternative One deserve a quick look before starting your walk. As you walk past a stonemason custom-making grave stones and statues, you will notice a stately temple located at the end of a road to the left. The temple, **Zuirin-ji** 瑞林寺 ㉗, is one of the biggest in the Yanaka area and is known for the grave of **Okubo Monto** 大久保主人, a seventeenth-century retainer of Shogun Ieyasu and pioneer of Edo's drinking-water system. Supplying water to hundreds of thousands of people was a major problem and the mission was given to Okubo, who had been in service to Ieyasu from his youth. Okubo embarked on a big project to channel the water of Inokashira Pond to the Kanda River, drawing from Zempuku-ji Pond and Myosho-ji Pond on the way. From the Kanda River, the water was supplied to various communities by conduits. Okubo died in 1617 and was buried at this temple. Take a stone path by the belfry. At its end is the Okubo family graveyard with a dozen antiquated gravestones.

Backtrack to the main road, go left and then right. At the next crossing, bear left. Soon, the black tiled roofs of another impressive temple, **Ichijo-ji** 一乗寺 ㉘, can be seen to your right. The temple is situated at a crossing with a traffic light on a busy road. Cross to the other side and turn right. About ten buildings away from the light is a small Japanese brush shop, **Tanabe Bunkaido** 田辺文魁堂 ㉙. This small shop belongs to the finest maker of calligraphy brushes in Japan. Pablo Piccaso and Joan Miro heard of the shop's high reputation and bought some. Facsimilies of these purchases are proudly exhibited in the small display window, along with several made of human hair. The old man who made them has passed away, but his son has inherited the skill. Continuing along the busy road, you will pass a fire station and then find **Tokuoken** 得応軒 ㉚, selling pigments and brushes for Japanese painting. The pigments used in Japanese painting are crushed rocks and seashells. The finer the particles are, the paler the hues. Mixed with glue and water, they are applied to the glazed surface of paper or silk.

Still keeping straight, past two traffic lights, you will arrive at the intersection with Shinobazu-dori. On the way, you can enjoy the various kinds of shops which come alive in the late afternoon and evening. The area along this part of the main road forms a shopping center named the Nezu Ginza, where a great variety of fresh food is sold. Visitors who like sushi, but are afraid of offending against etiquette, will appreciate the single-price system at **Kei** けい ㉛, a small place around the second corner to the right after Daikoku-ya *sembei* shop. Kei is operated by a Japanese who married an American woman, and every piece of sushi costs ¥180.

The subway entrance is on the other side of the major intersection.

Yanaka o aruku no wa omoshiroi desho?
(Isn't it fun to walk in Yanaka?)

TSUKIJI

Walking time
Tsukiji–Tsukudajima: 1 hour
The fish market depends on your schedule
Tsukiji–Hama Detached Palace Garden–Shimbashi: 1 hour

BACKGROUND Within an easy walk of fifteen minutes from the Ginza, Tsukiji is renowned for its bustling fish market, one of the largest in the world. The dynamism of its daily transactions, involving more than sixty-thousand market workers and shoppers, is absolutely overwhelming.

The market was moved here in 1931, and is a relatively new addition to the history of Tsukiji, which was reclaimed from the sea in the seventeenth century. The reclaimed land was originally used for the site of a prestigious temple and suburban residences of high-ranking lords, but just before the Meiji era, the area was made into a residential area for foreign traders and missionaries. A modern hospital of American origin now stands on the site of the foreign concession, and the three-hundred-year-old temple still maintains its commanding presence.

GETTING THERE Take the Hibiya Line to Tsukiji and ascend the stairway closest to Higashi Ginza.

A huge Indian-style edifice, **Tsukiji Hongan-ji** 築地本願寺 ①, can be seen in front of the subway exit. The temple's neighborhood, including the several blocks to your right and the central market ahead, is actually land reclaimed from the sea in

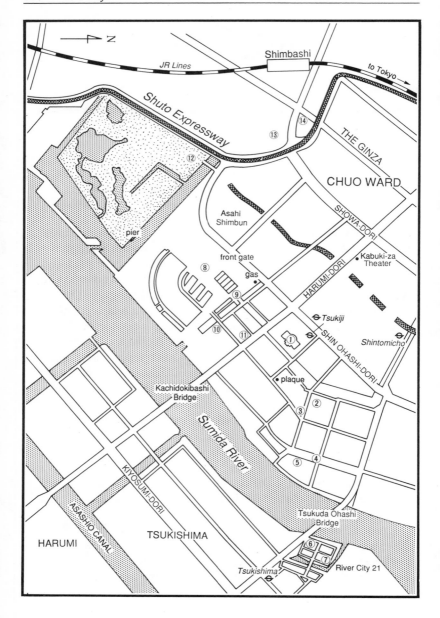

the seventeenth century and named Tsukiji, which literally means "constructed land."

A branch of Kyoto's Nishi Hongan-ji, Tsukiji Hongan-ji used to have a much bigger compound with more than fifty subsidiary temples under its control. The original building was a traditional structure with a large tiled roof visible from off-shore, serving as a good landmark for sailors. The present temple was designed by Dr. Chuta Ito who was inspired by the arts of ancient India and the Orient. Ito chose Horyu-ji temple in Nara as the theme of his graduation thesis, focusing on the influence of both Persian and Asian cultures on ancient Japan. In further pursuit of the origin of Japanese culture, he under-took several trips to China, India, Turkey, and Egypt. Ito's en-counter with Tenshin Okakura in 1893 led to one of his greatest contributions—a law for the preservation of old temples and shrines, which was the predecessor of the present Cultural Properties Protection Act.

In creating Hongan-ji, Ito was influenced by the arts of In-dia, the cradle of Buddhism, which shows in the exotic exterior design. The building is open to the public except when it is be-ing used for funerals and other purposes. Every year, on the Sunday closest to April 8, the temple celebrates Lord Buddha's birthday with a costumed children's procession and a fair in the compound *(from 10:00–15:00)*.

TOKYO'S FIRST FOREIGN SETTLEMENT Leaving the temple through the front gate, turn right. At the traffic light, cross the street and turn right. Just before the next traffic light, the road rises slightly where a bridge used to span a canal, but the waterway has since been filled in. A metal plaque, set into a stone stand on the other end of the former bridge, gives an im-pression of the foreign settlement which was located here in the early years of the Meiji era. Walk into the refurbished area on your left, with trees and a shallow artificial stream running on one side. Soon, there is another former bridge. Diagonally across to the right is **St. Luke's International Hospital**

聖路加国際病院 ②. Cross to the right and walk to a small triangular section of the next intersection. Two **granite memorials** ③ are placed there to commemorate the growth of modern medical science and a college in this area. The taller stone at the back is dedicated to three samurai doctors, Maeno Ryotaku, Sugita Genpaku, and Nakagawa Junan, who collaborated from 1771 to 1774 in translating a Dutch book on human anatomy. All three, each in the service of a different lord, happened to participate in the dissection of an executed criminal. They were amazed at the accuracy of the little-known Western anatomy book which they had read and translated in the days when Japan was closed to foreigners. They often worked at Maeno's house in the compound of Lord Okudaira's residence, which now belongs to St. Luke's Hospital. The other memorial is also related to Lord Okudaira's residence. A low-ranking samurai under Lord Okudaira, Fukuzawa Yukichi, started a private class in 1858 for the study of Western science and the Dutch language. Later named Keio Gijuku, it evolved into one of the leading colleges in Japan. In the stone book are engraved the famous words by Fukuzawa, "Heaven created no man above another, nor below." This was an extremely democratic concept to advocate at a time when the Tokugawa Shogunate, enfeebled though it was, still held sway. This bold statement spread like a thunderbolt, encouraging millions of people to stand up for freedom against the irrationalities of the feudal system. Now cross the street to St. Luke's Hospital and walk straight between the two buildings.

After Yoshinobu, the last shogun, resigned, and imperial rule was restored, the Meiji government cleared this area of the mansions of feudal lords and built colonial-style wooden houses for foreign diplomats and missionaries. This was a necessary consequence of the signing of the U.S.–Japan Commerce Treaty in 1858 and the subsequent opening of Japan to foreign powers. As many as nineteen countries and thirteen Christian denominations were represented here. St Luke's Hospital is an outgrowth of an American missionary group from that time. It was founded by Dr. Rudolf Teusler, who came in 1901 from Richmond, Virginia and introduced the American system of medical care. Near the east entrance of the current hospital, an inscription is set into the wall expressing the hospital's dedication to Christianity, in both English and Japanese. The other missions, too, developed various activities, including the foundation of schools, which grew into prestigious institutions such as St. Paul's College, Meiji Gakuin University, and St. Joseph School, now located elsewhere in Tokyo.

Turn right at the next intersection. Walk straight on and cross the main road at the next traffic light. Notice a square **stone memorial** 指紋研究発祥の地 ④, placed among the bushes on the right. It is dedicated to Henry Faulds, a Scottish Presbyterian missionary who lived here from 1874 to 1887 and who was a pioneer in fingerprinting research. During his stay in Japan, he became interested in the study of fingerprints, probably through the Japanese commoners' custom of using thumb prints for seals on documents and from traces of fingerprints left in ancient pottery which Dr. E.S. Morse excavated in Omori. In 1880, Dr. Faulds contributed an article to *Nature* magazine, mentioning the possible use of fingerprints in the identification of criminals.

The block ahead to the right is the site of the **U.S. Legation** アメリカ公使館跡 ⑤, which is being redeveloped into modern medical facilities. Continue past the Henry Faulds memorial, turn left and walk to the end of the street where it crosses with another street. This second street rises to the right to become a bridge to cross the Sumida River. If you turn left here and walk straight on, you will find the entrance to Shintomicho Station on the Yurakucho line subway. For now, however, cross the street and turn right to walk toward the bridge. By a stairway near the concrete wall bordering the river, a stone post stands in commemoration of a ferry service which used to carry people across the river until the bridge, Tsukuda Ohashi, was built in 1961. Ascend the steps and stop for a while on the pedestrian walkway.

The Sumida River is quite broad here as Tokyo Bay is just beyond Kachidokibashi bridge, off to the right. To your left, yet another bridge, Eitaibashi, can be seen in the distance. Tall office buildings rise along both riverbanks, creating a scene reminiscent of Hong Kong. This is one of the places where Tokyo changed most drastically in the late 1980s. The traditional warehouse and factory districts have been replaced by office buildings for banks and brokerage houses. Thus, IBM, Mitsui, Mitsubishi, Sumitomo, Nomura, and a host of other leading companies rushed to the riverside and bay areas where large spaces were available to accommodate their high-tech transaction systems.

The skyscrapers on the right-hand bank are apartments developed on the site of Ishikawajima Harima Heavy Industries Company. The location was originally an island, Ishikawajima, where the company originated as a shipbuilder. The redevelopment of the factory site is a large project named River City 21. In order to prevent speculative purchases, the apartments are available for lease only.

TSUKUDAJIMA ISLAND   To the right of the aparment towers, the geometric red gate is a sluice for a narrow inlet of the Sumida River. Further to its right stands a greyish green torii. Low buildings surrounding the shrine gate form the community of **Tsukudajima** 佃島 ⑥, which also used to be an island.

As you reach the end of the bridge, you can sometimes smell soy sauce. The aroma comes from the shops with big roof signs in kanji on your left. *Tsukudani* (small fish and seaweed boiled down in soy sauce) is being made. This seafood speciality is named after the former island and used to be a very common addition to rice in the daily meals of the Japanese.

At the end of the bridge, go down the stairway, make a U-turn to the left and go right. The street is soon crossed by another street. These two streets, short as they are, made up the main streets of the former island. Because it escaped destruction in the Great Earthquake of 1923 and in the air raids during

World War II, the basic street plan has remained basically un-changed since the Edo period. The *tsukudani* shops have been in business since the Edo period. One of them, **Tenyasu** 天安, has an attractive square lantern in front displaying the shop's name.

Walking to the end of the first street, you will come to the green torii you saw from the bridge. It marks the riverside en-trance to a shrine, **Sumiyoshi-jinja** 住吉神社 ⑦, visible off to the right. The shrine is dedicated to the tutelary god of the first settlers who came here in the late sixteenth century. Originally based at a village called Tsukuda, in Settsu (Osaka), they helped Tokugawa Ieyasu in a battle before he became shogun. Ieyasu later invited them to Edo and gave them the exclusive right to fish in Edo Bay and sell the catch at Nihombashi. Tak-ing pride in their special relationship with the shogun, the vil-lagers had their shrine directed toward Edo Castle and erected tall banners high by the riverside during their annual festival so that the shogun could see them. They also started a tradition of carrying the shrine's *omikoshi* through the torii into the Sumida River. This tradition continued until 1962.

As you enter through the second torii, you will notice a cov-ered fountain where you can wash your hands. The carved decorations under the roof are considered to date from the late nineteenth century. Behind the fountain is **Katsuozuka,** a large inscribed monolith which is a monument dedicated to the bo-nito, a very popular fish in the Edo period. The shrine's festival takes place every three years in early August, and is a large affair for such a small community of a little over three-hundred households. The three-day program features a highly ani-mated parade of large lion heads on the first day, an *omikoshi* parade to Kachidokibashi on the second day, and another *omikoshi* parade through the neighboring districts on the third day. Throughout, a lively festival music floats from four stands on the island, and six tall banners flutter in the summer wind. The millions of yen needed to finance the festival are donated by the residents. The unflagging enthusiasm of the islanders led to the revival of the carrying of the shrine's *omikoshi* into the Sumida River in 1990, not on people's shoulders as it used to be, but onboard a barge.

Leave the shrine from an exit to the right of the main building. As you walk, look into the narrow alleys between the tenement houses which are built in the same dimensions from the Edo period, except that they are now two-storied. Plants and flowers in pots, plastic tubs, and buckets fill the space between the alleys and house fronts. Tending the potted plants is an important part of daily life here.

At the next crossing, stop and look to your right. This street, which is the second of the two main streets of Tsukudajima, is the stage for another special summer event. The people of the island present a unique *bon odori* (group dance). The occasion is Obon, a festival to pray for the happiness of the souls of the ancestors. The unique *bon odori* of Tsukudajima has been designated an intangible cultural asset by the Tokyo Metropolitan Government. It takes place on the evenings of July 13, 14, and 15, between 7:00 and 9:00 P.M., with both children and adults participating; a little before 8:00 P.M. is the best time to arrive, when the children are finishing and the adults beginning. White paper lanterns are lit in doorways, and a man on a raised wooden platform sings old songs over and over again to a monotonous drum beat. At the end of the street is placed an altar to which people pray before joining in the circle of dancers. The atmosphere is very spiritual because they are supposed to be dancing with the souls of the dead who return home once a year. The dolorous melodies, accentuated by drum beats, have a hypnotic charm which takes you back to olden times. Leave before the dance has ended and walk back across the bridge. The man's singing voice carries across the big river and will follow you all the way. Looking back, the lantern-lit platform can be seen looming above the dark rooflines, while the rest of the town is lulled by deepening shadows of evening—an unforgettable scene which will impress visitors with a strong sense of the underlying spiritual tradition in Japanese culture.

To the left of the crossing, the small main street leads to a red bridge across a canal. If you go one short block beyond the bridge, you will reach the border of what was once the former island, but which is now connected to Tsukishima and Harumi by landfill. The view from the red bridge presents an interesting contrast of the old and new. Increased use of modern materials and designs has lessened the otherworldliness of Tsukudajima, but the sight is still enough to make you wonder if this is part of Tokyo. Skyscrapers rise in the distance, an old shrine nestles in the woods, and traditional *yakatabune* boats are moored along with steel fishing boats.

If you walk straight from the bridge and turn right, you will come to a highway, where you will find the subway entrance to Tsukishima Station on the Yurakucho Line. Otherwise, walk back to Tsukuda Ohashi bridge for either Shintomicho or Tsukiji stations.

TSUKIJI FISH MARKET – HAMA RIKYU

TSUKIJI CENTRAL MARKET 築地中央市場 ⑧, which is the largest fish market in the Orient, is a public facility managed and supervised by the Tokyo Metropolitan Government. The market comes alive at 2:00 A.M. to prepare for the auctions which begin at 5:00 A.M. and continue throughout the morning. Every morning the huge market bustles with people and trucks moving around at a mad pace. You may not be prepared for the slippery ground and heavy traffic, but the amazing variety of seafood and the excitement of the scene will make it worthwhile. The best time to visit the market depends on your purpose—whether you are going to see the auctions, just to look around, or to shop. The auctions are held in several places in the market at different times according to the type of product. Be sure to watch the tuna auction which begins at 5:50 A.M., but plan to arrive a little before that time. If you are planning to shop, go around 9:30 to 10:00 A.M. to the wholesale market, and between 9:00 and noon to the retail area called *jōgai* or "outside market." By this time, the professional buyers will have finished shopping, and the vendors will be more relaxed and helpful to ordinary shoppers.

In 1991, a twelve-year project to renovate the fifty-year-old buildings commenced. Reconstruction is proceeding in a chain of partial demolition and construction, to eventually produce a three-story market surrounded by buildings up to twenty-seven stories high with offices, parking, and storage facilities. The total market space will more than double, and parking will increase by 35 percent. One major reason for the reconstruction is the rapid increase in import of fish and marine produce since the mid-1980s. Large containers packed with frozen and chilled shrimp and tuna arrive at Narita, making the airport a major "fishing port." After customs clearance, these are carried by fleets of trucks to Tsukiji and other wholesale markets in Japan. Vegetables and fruit, too, come from abroad to fill sizable portions of the domestic market. *(For general information call Kōhō-ka, the Publicity Section of the Central Market. Tel: 3542-1111 ex. 4343.)*

To get to the tuna auction, cross the street from Tsukiji Station to Honganji temple and turn right. Walk straight on, crossing the major intersection and passing numerous small shops and eating stalls along the main street. Cross a bridge and turn left at the corner of a gas station. You will be walking to the end of this road, but notice a **small shrine** ⑨ inside a high metal fence on the left, about midway down the road. When you reach the end of the road, turn right. The tuna auction takes place on your left. Within this open space, you will see the spectacular sight of hundreds of frozen tuna laid on the ground.

Another interesting part of the market is the restaurant section. Walk back to the small shrine mentioned earlier. At the shrine, turn left instead of keeping straight. On the right are several alleys lined with small restaurants, including sushi bars, coffee shops, and kitchen supply shops. If you take the third right, you will find **Aiyo Coffee** 愛養コーヒー in the sec-

ond unit. Beyond it, in the seventh unit, is **Daiwa Sushi** 大和寿
司, which is used to foreign guests. Going back to the little
shrine, turn right at the end of the road. A tea shop on the right,
called **Sankyu** 三久, has a very friendly salesman who loves to
pour a cup of tea for you; *gemmai-cha* (green tea mixed with
roasted brown rice) and *hōji-cha* (aromatic brown tea) are very
popular.

Walk through the roofed arcade and cross the bridge on
your left. The bridge separates the wholesale market from the
jōgai retail area. On the right is **Namiyoke-jinja** 波除神社⑩, a
shrine popular with market people. The shrine's annual festival on June 8 is well known for its lively *omikoshi* parade. To the
left of the shrine are more than six hundred small shops
crammed along mazelike alleys, each specializing in meat,
pickles, vegetables, tea, nuts and crackers, pottery, lacquerware, baskets, and cutlery in addition to fresh and frozen fish.

If you turn right after leaving the shrine and walk straight
on, you will come out to a highway, Harumi-dori. Turn left
here. Several buildings away from the corner is **Totoya** ととや
⑪ , which serves good *yakitori* on rice. Look for a blue *noren*
with the kanji for bird in the center (鳥). Ask for *teishoku*. (*Open
9:00-13:00. Closed on Sundays and holidays.*) If you continue
straight past it, you will come back to the first major intersection which you crossed to go to the tuna auction. The pottery
shops near the intersection carry good items.

To take a leisurely stroll through a spacious daimyo garden,
turn left at the intersection and keep straight on, passing the
front gate of the central market on the left and the Asahi Shim-
bun head office on the right. Soon a bridge is seen spanning a
canal on the left. The bridge leads to the entrance of **Hama Detached Palace Garden** 浜離宮庭園⑫ . To enter the garden, a
small admission is charged. This used to be the suburban residence of the great Tokugawa family. Take any path in the garden, but remember to return to the original gate when you
leave. The path to the left leads to a pier, from which you can
take a cruise up the Sumida River to Asakusa. Of the three

ponds in the garden, the smaller two are specially walled-in areas for duck hunting and are kept as natural as possible. The large pond in the center of the garden used to be a tidal pool which let the seawater in. Many graceful buildings used to dot the attractive landscape, but were bombed during World War II. The most elegant house, which stood on the island in the center of the large pond, has recently been reproduced, complete with a terrace projecting out over the water. It was here that U.S. President Ulysses S. Grant had an audience with Emperor Meiji in 1879. This building can be rented for parties and meetings. *(Call 3541-0200 for information.)*

Leaving the garden, walk across the pedestrian bridge and go straight on. Ascend the next pedestrian bridge and turn left to cross over the street below. Walk straight away from the bridge. The big compound on your left is the JR **Shiodome Cargo Station** 汐留貨物駅跡 ⑬ which is going to be developed, possibly into a financial service center, in the near future. This site was the original Shimbashi Station where Japan's first railroad service was inaugurated. A marker with the number '0' and a section of the original rails are preserved to commemorate the starting point of the old trains leaving for Yokohama.

This course thus ends at zero. Straight ahead and to the left is the JR Shimbashi Station. If you turn right at the next intersection, you will be on the Ginza. At this crossing is **Hashizen** 橋善 ⑭, a good tempura restaurant dating back to the Edo period, famous for its *kakiage* served on rice.

Ichiba wa dō deshita ka?
(How did you like the market?)

Design detail of Nezu-jinja   *photograph by Atsushi Matsushima*

Stone lanterns
at Kanei-ji, Ueno
courtesy Taito Ward

Pagoda of Kanei-ji, ▶
Ueno
courtesy Taito Ward

Bank of Japan
courtesy Chuo Ward

Summer festival of Tomioka Hachiman, Fukagawa
courtesy Koto Ward

Donto festival of Torigoe-jinja, Kuramae   *courtesy Taito Ward* ▶

Portable shrine
on the Sumida River
courtesy Chuo Ward

Old Shitamachi
house, Yanaka
courtesy Taito Ward

Cherry-blossom viewing on the Sumida riverside
courtesy Sumida Ward

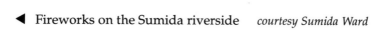

◀ Fireworks on the Sumida riverside   *courtesy Sumida Ward*

SHINAGAWA

Walking time
Sengaku-ji–Shinagawa: 30 minutes
Shinagawa–Shimbanba: 1 hour

BACKGROUND   If you are interested in contrasting the culture of the samurai with the commoners' way of life, try this course. Even now, Shinagawa retains its contrast between the temples and samurai residences on the heights and the bustling commercial activities of the commoners below.

A large tract of land by Shinagawa Station is slated for an ambitious redevelopment which will add to the drastic changes the area has already undergone. However, the traces of history which remain here and there make the area worth investigating.

GETTING THERE   Take the Yamanote Line to Gotanda. At Gotanda, descend the stairway in the middle of the platform and, after passing through the ticket gate, turn left. Outside the station to the left is the entrance to the Toei Asakusa subway station. Descend the stairs and take the train from track 2 to Sengakuji Station, which is two stops away. At Sengakuji, ascend the stairway near the front of the train and go right after passing through the ticket gate, and take Exit A4 to come out on the street.

To the left on the main street is the site of the most important checkpoint on the Tokaido Highway (now Route 15) 高輪大木

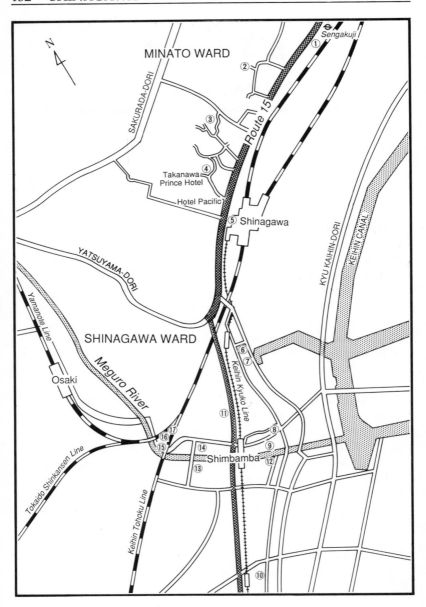

MINATO WARD

① Sengakuji

②

SAKURADA-DORI

Route 15

③

④ Takanawa
Prince Hotel

Hotel Pacific

⑤ Shinagawa

KYU KAIHIN-DORI

KEIHIN CANAL

YATSUYAMA-DORI

Yamanote Line

SHINAGAWA WARD

Meguro River

Osaki

Keihin Kyuko Line

⑥
⑦

⑪

⑧

⑨

⑰
⑯
⑮

⑭

⑫

Shimbamba

⑬

Tokaido Shinkansen Line

Keihin Tohoku Line

⑩

戸跡 ①. Of the major highways radiating from Edo, the Tokaido was the busiest and most important. During the Edo period, high walls stopped travelers from sneaking through, but all that remains of the former checkpoint is a mound of earth surrounded by several pine trees. This gate was the first checkpoint on the Tokaido for travelers leaving Edo and the last for those entering the city. It was here that every traveler had his or her baggage and traveling papers closely examined. The investigation was very strict, particularly for "outgoing women and incoming guns," and it sometimes took a few days before clearance was given.

Continue walking straight along the main street. At the next traffic light, where another street joins the main street at a T-junction, turn right and walk toward the green-roofed gate of **Sengaku-ji** 泉岳寺 ②. The temple is famous for the tombs of Lord Asano and his forty-seven samurai. The story of the forty-seven samurai is based on an actual incident which took place in 1702, later to be immortalized in countless Kabuki and Bun-raku plays. The story began when an imperial envoy from Kyoto was expected at Edo Castle. For reasons not quite clear, Lord Asano drew his sword in protest against a senior lord, Kira, during preparations for the envoy's reception. The draw-ing of swords in the castle was forbidden by law, and because of this, Asano was sentenced to death, and his fief was confis-cated by the shogun. No one else was punished. To Asano's loyal men, this was a traumatic loss. Unable to persuade the shogunate to punish the other lord involved in the incident, a group of the now masterless samurai, taking matters into their own hands, ambushed and killed Lord Kira. Since revenge kill-ings were also forbidden, they were sentenced to death.

Inside the gate stands a statue of Oishi Kuranosuke, the samurai leader, holding a scroll containing an oath to revenge the death of Lord Asano. Most of the temple buildings were lost during World War II and have recently been rebuilt. The second gate of the temple, however, dates from 1836 and has an old metalwork dragon on the ceiling. The museum to the left of the main building contains the clothes, armor, and other personal belongings of the forty-seven samurai and their lord, as well as wooden statues depicting them. Follow the red arrow to your left to see their graves.

Leaving the temple from the front gate, turn right and walk to the end of the road. Just before the road runs into a garage, turn left to go back to the main street. On the corner is the Dai-Ichi Kangyo Bank. Turn right and walk to the next traffic light. Cross the street toward the brown building of Futaba Company and turn right to walk uphill. Thickly wooded estates remain on both sides, though some have been replaced by modern condominiums. Immediately past a gate with antiquated lamps on stone poles, take a paved lane to the left. (If this turning point is difficult to find, go back to the main street and continue walking until you come to a crossing with a pedestrian bridge just beyond. Turn right and walk along a street lined with willow trees to the front gate of the next temple.) The secret path rises at first and then descends as it curves to the left and right. Soon, it meets another narrow road bordered by the low beige wall of **Tozenji** 東禅寺 ③ , your next destination. A beautiful, newly erected three-story pagoda can be seen on the right.

Continue downhill and around to the right to reach the main entrance. The simple gate and neatly trimmed trees along the approach are very refreshing. In a spacious compound, the main building with its simple but powerful style reflects its character as a prestigious Zen temple. High on the facade is a wooden frame with four characters written in strong, fluid strokes signifying from left to right sea, above, Zen, forest. Altogether, they describe the temple as it was during the Edo period, when the sea could be seen close to the bottom of this hill. This stately building was used as the British Legation between 1859 and 1873.

From the temple's front gate, walk straight ahead. Just before the main street, there is a park on the right, with a low modern waterfall in the foreground. Turn right there and follow a path along the left side of the park. At the end, ascend the steps on your left. You will find yourself facing the banquet building of the **Takanawa Prince Hotel** 高輪プリンスホテル ④, which stands on the site of Prince Takeda's residence, famous for its beautiful garden. Turn left, passing an early twentieth-century Western-style building and descend a winding path to the main street.

At the main street, turn right and walk over a pedestrian bridge. If you look to your left at the top of the overpass, Shinagawa Station is beyond. In front of the station, a **stone memorial** ⑤ by the sidewalk along the main street commemorates Japan's first railway service started in 1872. This station was the original starting point of the rail service, preceding the official opening of the railway between Shimbashi and Yokohama.

The railway project was supervised by a group of British engineers under the guidance of Edmund Morel, who served as chief engineer. Morel emphasized the training of local people and used as much domestic material as possible. For instance, he noticed the abundant supply of quality wood in Japan and encouraged its use. Thus, the first bridge on the Tama River was built of *hinoki* (Japanese cypress), and the ties to support the tracks were also made from Japanese wood. Unfortunately he died of tuberculosis at the early age of twenty nine in 1871, without seeing the completion of his project. His tombstone in the Foreign Cemetery in Yokohama uses the design of a train ticket at the top, bordered by cross sections of old tracks. The tombstone was installed in 1934 as a gift from a Japanese railway fan in appreciation of the British engineer's dedicated work. His tomb had been ignored for a long time, particularly after the Great Earthquake of 1923, which caused severe damage to the whole cemetery. The restored tomb receives the homage of Japan Railway every year on October 14. John Diack, another British engineer on the project, who drove in the zero marker at Shimbashi Station, lived to the age of seventy-two. He is buried in the same cemetery, and there is an inscription on his tombstone which reads, "Thy will be done."

Past Shinagawa Station, continue along the main street until you come to an arched railroad and pedestrian bridge which goes over the tracks on your left. Cross the bridge on the right-hand side and then turn right. Soon cross the street to the left to enter another street which gradually descends. This street, with many shops on both sides, is part of the old Tokaido depicted in Hiroshige's print of Shinagawa. As you walk, look to your left. You will notice a sudden drop in the land level because the lower area was in the sea in Hiroshige's time. Bustling inns and entertainment houses used to stand along this street and side lanes, all of which have been replaced by modern buildings. Except for several temples set back from the street, nothing remains to convey the mood of the old days. The street does come alive, however, in the late afternoon. Endless rows of small shops, with men calling aloud the day's best buy and housewives looking for inexpensive fresh ingredients for dinner, remind one of the lively town.

If you would like to sample the local food, I suggest **Kikusushi** 菊すし ⑥ , on the corner of the first road to the left. About twenty shops away from it is a *soba* restaurant, **Eiki-an** 栄亀庵 ⑦, which exhibits samples of its noodles in a window to the right of the entrance. Close to the first traffic light at the major intersection is another sushi restaurant, **Otomi** 大富 ⑧, which serves good sushi at reasonable prices. Take the street to the right just before the traffic light. The restaurant is four shops from the corner on the left, with lanterns and a large display case at the entrance.

The area is all the more animated during its annual festival in June. Various makeshift stalls are put up in shopfronts, and houses are decorated with colorful lanterns and ornaments. "Shinagawa Byoshi," a cheerful tune from this area, is played at a quick tempo and brightens people's hearts. Dressed in festival costume, residents gather at the tutelary shrine near the river ahead. Cross the major intersection and walk straight to a bridge which spans the Meguro River. The shrine, **Ebara-jinja**

荏原神社 ⑨, nestles in woods a little off to the right. There is, however, a temple which deserves a look if you have time. The temple has a large bronze statue of Jizo which was installed in 1708 as one of the Six Jizo of Edo placed along the seventeenth-century city boundaries. Keep straight on for about ten minutes, passing two more traffic lights. The temple, **Honsenji** 品川寺 ⑩, on the right of the street, is the home of the nine-foot-tall, cast-metal Jizo. All over his body, the lotus, and stone pedestal are inscribed small characters representing the names of thousands of donors who gave their pennies to erect this statue.

Inside the temple's gate are an old gingko tree and a cinnabar-painted main hall. A large bell in the belfry, dated 1657, went missing for many years after it was exhibited at the Paris Exposition in 1867. By chance, it was located in a museum in Geneva, Switzerland, and was returned to Japan in 1930.

Retrace your steps to the bridge and proceed to Ebara-jinja. Enveloped in thick foliage, Ebara-jinja is one of the largest religious establishments in this area; founded in the ninth century, the shrine has a beautifully decorated main building with carved birds and waves. Its annual festival falls on the weekend closest to June 7. On the last day of the festival the shrine's *omikoshi* is carried by boat down to the sea. At the shore, a company of boisterous bearers shoulder it and wade through the shallow water. This rite is based on a legend that long ago when the sea reached closer, a farmer found the mask of a god on the shore and gave it to the shrine. The head priest then had a dream in which it was revealed that because the mask had been cast up from the sea, it should occasionally be taken back and bathed in the sea water. When this was done, the villagers had an unusually good catch of fish and seaweed. Another old shrine nearby, **Shinagawa-jinja** 品川神社 ⑪, also holds a festival on these days. This shrine still preserves many vestiges of its early history, including a seventeenth-century torii, old lanterns, and masks used for the Kagura dances in April and September. The neighborhood of Ebara-jinja is busy in November also, on the occasion of Tori-no Ichi, the Lucky Rake Fair day.

Leaving the shrine, cross the bridge with the knobbed railing. Turn right and walk on the left-hand side of the street. Shortly, when you come to the next bridge on the right, on the left is a wooden gate which is the side entrance to **Kaitoku-ji** 海徳寺 ⑫, a temple with an attractive 250-year-old main building. Note the subtle curve of the roof and the carvings of a dragon and a phoenix in the center with two guardian dogs on either side. A human figure holds up the central roof beam, as seen in some Roman architecture, but a very rare feature in a Japanese building. Built without nails, the temple is marvelously resistant to earthquakes. At the time of the Great Earthquake, the lower parts of the wooden pillars near the front entrance slid forward half an inch or so, leaving them slightly off center.

Leave through the front gate opposite the main building and turn right. At the next crossing, turn right, and walk all the way down to the main street, Route 15. If you wish to go home at this point, Shimbanba Station on the Keihin Kyuko Line is a little off to your right under the railroad overpass. From this station you can get on a train (track 2) to Shinagawa on the Yamanote Line or to Mita for transfer to the Toei Mita Line.

After crossing Route 15, go straight past the black gate of a temple on the right and along its side wall. Past a few more buildings, take the first right. A little before a bridge which is seen ahead is the gate of **Seiko-in** 清光院 ⑬. Enter for a look at an unusual old cemetery. In front of the main building which is on the left, there is a small but pretty garden with some stone lanterns and a gazebo. In the far left-hand corner of the graveyard is the cemetery of Lord Okudaira's family, surrounded by walls of piled-up roof tiles.

The Okudaira were a prestigious family descended from their first generation head, who was married to a daughter of Shogun Ieyasu. Walking inside the half-crumbled gate, you may feel as if you have blundered into a world totally isolated from the present. Rows of imposing stone tombs, many of which are more than ten feet high, overwhelm you with their bleak and massive silence. The older ones are constructed of five differently shaped stones which bear five kanji characters, representing from the bottom upward earth, water, fire, wind, and the void. This style is called *gorin-no-tō* and was used for the tombs of high-class samurai from the thirteenth century. The oldest *gorin-no-tō* here, which date back to the mid-seventeenth century, are the three huge ones in the middle row on the right. These, along with the stone gate and wall of the cemetery, retain the early Edo style of a daimyo cemetery. Precious relics that they are, it is interesting to compare these tombs with the small bas-reliefs in Yanaka. These grand but rigid monuments seem void of the intimate sentiments expressed by the commoners in their little stone memorials. Adjacent to the Okudaira cemetery is a burial place for the Nagai family, who were also high-ranking samurai. About five-dozen large individual tombstones are equally impressive, but somehow look more modern compared with the weathered tombs of the Okudairas.

From Seiko-in, turn right to cross the bridge over the Meguro River and walk to the traffic light at a T-junction. There is a children's park with concrete dinosaurs on the left-hand corner of the crossing. On the right is a Mitsubishi automobile sales office, next to which is the entrance to **Tokai-ji** 東海寺 ⑭, another Zen temple founded in the Edo period. The approach to the temple is lined with cedar trees and is always swept clean. The present building is actually a former subsidiary of the temple. (Seiko-in, too, was a subsidiary of the same temple.) Close to the belfry with its bell cast in 1692, stands a beautiful wooden hall with slatted doors and windows housing a statue of Buddha surrounded by attendant bodhisattvas and saints. A modern granite monument nearby recalls the atom-bombing of Hiroshima and Nagasaki. A group of *hibakusha* (survivors of the bombing) living in Tokyo were concerned that memory of the disaster was fading and erected the stone engraved with a message. Off to the left are the main building and attached living quarters for the abbots of the temple. The serene atmosphere of these buildings seems to mirror the moral integrity of the temple's founder and generations of his descendants.

The original Tokai-ji was the third most important temple in Edo, after Kanei-ji in Ueno and Zojo-ji in Shiba. It was built by the third shogun, Iemitsu, in 1638 and was given to the Zen abbot Takuan. Its compound was about forty-one acres, but most of the land was diverted for use by factories and schools after the Meiji Restoration.

Takuan was born in 1573 and entered the priesthood at the age of ten. After years of disciplined practice, he became the head priest of Daitoku-ji in Kyoto at age thirty-seven. However, he fell from favor and was exiled to northern Japan by the shogunate for his fierce resistance to the state's meddling in religious affairs. After intercession by his powerful friends, he was eventually released and offered the abbotship of Tokai-ji by Shogun Iemitsu. To most, the name *takuan* is better known as a kind of pickled daikon which the priest invented. The pickle is made from a whole daikon (about 2 feet long) which is pickled in salt and rice bran and pressed under a stone.

Leaving Tokai-ji, turn left, cross the street, and turn left again. The street curves to the left and then to the right. Just past the railroad overpass is a brownish-red square stone monument. It indicates the site of the first glassware factory built here in 1873 官営品川硝子製作所跡 ⑮ and is witness to the first stage of Japan's industrialization in the early Meiji era. Cut-glass techniques taught here by British craftsmen started a tradition of Edo-style cut glass which has been preserved. Parts of the original factory's brick buildings have been moved to the Meiji-mura Park in Inuyama City.

A narrow cement path on your right, between the JR railway tracks and the building of Sankyo Pharmaceutical Company which now stands on the site of the glass factory, leads to **Takuan's tomb** 沢庵之墓 ⑯, which is up a flight of steps to a small hill. The tomb is designated a national cultural asset.

Descending the low hill, turn left and climb up a little further. Another tomb behind a stone torii is that of Kamo-no Mabuchi, an Edo-period classical scholar. Further back in the cemetery, in a triangular lot formed by the Yamanote and the Shinkansen lines, is the tomb of **Inoue Masaru** 井上勝墓 ⑰, the Japanese counterpart of Edmund Morel (mentioned earlier in this chapter) in the railway project. An arrow on a white wooden board bearing his name points to his burial place. Immediately beyond a small wooden gate is a tombstone of his descendants. At the end of a short stone path to the left is another stone indicating the burial place of Inoue and his wife. In 1863, before the Meiji Restoration, Inoue sneaked out of Japan illegally in order to study mining and railroads in England for five years. Shortly after his return to Japan in 1869 after the demise of the shogunate, he was appointed head of the railroad project by the Meiji government which had just been formed. Inoue and Morel strove hard to overcome the countless technical and managerial problems which threatened the completion of the project. Inoue pursued the subsequent plans to build a nationwide network of railroads. It was very fortunate for Japan that these two men could work together at the beginning of the project. Inoue understood the importance of Morel's advice for the training of well-qualified, independent Japanese staff and devoted a great deal of his energy to the technical education needed to achieve this goal.

As you stand gazing at Inoue's tomb now, blue-and-white *shinkansen* (bullet trains) whisk past only a few yards away. On the other side, many local trains rattle to and fro.

Well, this is the end of this course. Walk back to the glass factory memorial and turn left to walk several minutes to Shimbanba Station, which is beyond Route 15. The entrance is to the left on the other side of the busy street.

Kisha no tabi wa suki desu ka?
(Do you like traveling by train?)

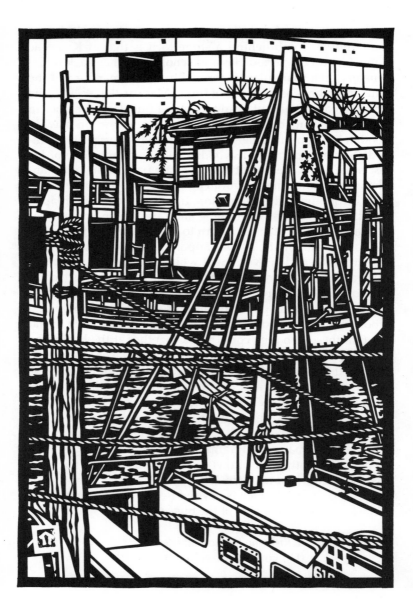

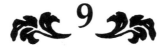

RYOGOKU–ASAKUSABASHI

Walking time
Ryogoku–Kuramae: 1 hour 30 minutes
Asakusabashi: 30 minutes

BACKGROUND Ryogoku is a sumo town on the east bank of the Sumida River, with a long history dating back to the seventeenth century when a bridge spanning the river and a large temple were built. The riversides prospered as a summer resort, popular for strolling, boating, and firework displays. The temple compound was licensed to hold sumo tournaments, which attracted crowds of visitors. In the Meiji era, a special domed building was erected in the temple compound to host the sumo tournaments, but this building has now been lost. After a lapse of nearly forty years during which sumo was moved to the west bank of the river, the national sport has once again moved back to this original area in a grand new building, built in 1984. Strolling through this area, you may chance upon some sumo wrestlers or eat a wrestlers' favorite food, *chanko nabe*, at a local restaurant.

After exploring the east bank, the course covers the west bank as well. Asakusabashi, where the course ends, developed around a crucial junction of the Sumida River and the spiral waterway which spread out from Edo Castle. Nowadays Asakusabashi is known as an interesting shopping area for dolls, toys, and Christmas decorations.

GETTING THERE The tour starts at Ryogoku Station on the JR Sobu Line. As your train approaches the station, you can see the enormous green roof of the Kokugikan Sumo Arena. Take

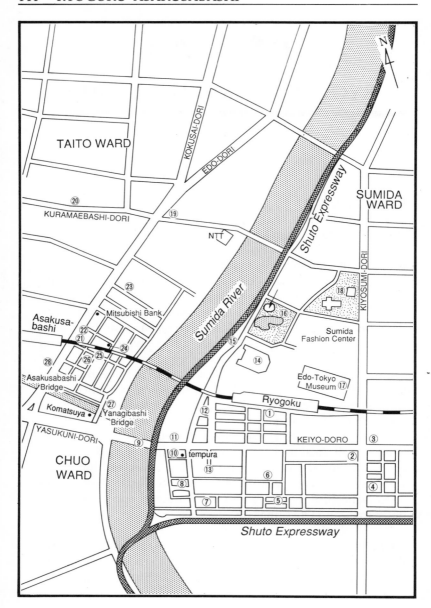

the stairway at the end (not middle) of the platform. After passing through the ticket gate, turn left, and then left again to walk along the street by the station building.

THE OLD SUMO TOWN   Sumo is the national sport of Japan, competing with baseball in popularity. Ryogoku was the cradle of the present style of tournament, established in the eighteenth century, and almost all the stables (institutions for the training of new wrestlers) used to be centered here. This historic concentration of sumo stables has given rise to a number of unique restaurants and shops in this area. However, high land prices are forcing many of the old and new stables out, leaving only about a dozen.

Near the next crossing with a street from the right is the **Tatsunami Stable** 立浪部屋 ①, housed in a modern building whose upper stories are used as apartments. To the right of the entrance, marked by a large wooden signboard carrying the stable's name, is a training hall with a ring. In January, May, September, December, and other times when the wrestlers are in town, you often see young wrestlers in their unique hairdo and *yukata*. When the window is open, you can peep in from the street to see them training during the morning.

Return to the main thoroughfare along the station and walk towards a crossing with a traffic light. Turn right to walk to the next traffic light. On the other side of the intersection is **Liondo** ライオン堂 ②, with a big horizontal shop sign depicting two sumo wrestlers squatting. The shop specializes in giant-size shirts and underwear. Cross the street to the left for a look at **Okada-ya** 岡田屋 ③ footwear shop in the third building from the corner. Oversized sandals and shoes are sold at this small shop, along with normal sizes. Back at the intersection, cross to the left and walk straight along the left side of the main road. **Kikuya** 喜久屋 ④ , a modest shop in the fourth block from the intersection, specializes in custom-made *tabi* (split-toe socks) and enjoys the patronage of sumo wrestlers. On a panel inside the shop, examples of jumbo footprints taken from the shop's order book are shown. Along with the huge feet of previous and current sumo wrestlers are those of John Wayne and the king of Tonga!

In the display window to the right, a brief history of *tabi* is given, using replicas of old and new styles. According to the description, *tabi* evolved from socks worn by aristocrats in ancient times. Around the thirteenth century, the divided-toe style spread along with the rise of samurai who wore *waraji* sandals with thongs between the toes. *Waraji* suited strenuous outdoor activities better than the loose sabot-like ancient shoes. Among the samurai, however, wearing tabi was a privilege allowed in winter only. Straps were used to tie *tabi* around the ankles, but these have been replaced by metal hooks. Ancient-style socks with undivided toes were used during the *Daijō-sai* ritual, part of the emperor's enthronement ceremony in November 1990, and this shop supplied a few hundred pairs of plain white ritual socks worn by the courtiers in the ceremony.

Cross the street at the traffic light near Kikuya and walk straight. You will notice that most residents run small businesses in apparel, parts-making, printing, and the like, often using their foyers as workshops or reception rooms for customers. Past another traffic light, in the second block, is the **Oshima Stable** 大島部屋 ⑤, in a drab gray building. A modest signboard is hung by a stairway, and a square cement plate embossed with a jumbo handprint is set on the facade. Past this building, take the next right to visit the site of **Lord Kira's house** 吉良邸跡 ⑥, which the forty-seven samurai attacked in 1702 to restore the honor of their lord (see page 133). All that remains is a small square space surrounded by plastered walls. On December 14 every year a festival is held here in the morning in honor of the brave deed. But in the afternoon, there is another celebration which commemorates how well Lord Kira governed his fief! The neighborhood becomes crowded with stalls selling winter clothes made by local manufacturers.

Continuing along the main road past another traffic light, you will pass by the **Izutsu Stable** 井筒部屋 ⑦, several buildings beyond a liquor shop on the left. The one-story front section with two slatted windows is obviously the training hall of the prosperous stable which has about thirty wrestlers. When you come to a T-junction, cross the street and turn right. Soon after turning, look to the left. You will notice a large gray building which has a green-gabled entrance like that of the Kokugikan. This is another prominent stable, the **Kasugano Stable** 春日野部屋 ⑧, which is the second largest of all. Continuing straight you will come to an intersection with a busy main road. Just before the intersection, on the left, **Tentomi** 天富, a charming tempura restaurant, has been in operation for over a hundred years. At the snug counter, you can relish piping hot tempura, just as it was served at street stalls during the Edo period. *Chanko nabe* is also served upon reservation. *(Open 11:30-13:00, 17:00-19:30 on weekdays. Closed on Sundays and national holidays. Reservations on Saturdays and weekday evenings only. Tel: 3631-0193.)*

At the Ryogoku 1-chome intersection, turn left for a quick look at the famous **Ryogokubashi bridge** 両国橋 ⑨. With the gigantic Shuto Expressway overhead, it is difficult to visualize the pleasure-laden atmosphere associated with the bridge and its neighborhoods during the Edo period. During the summer, rows of makeshift stalls, teahouses, and show huts were in business until midnight and always bustled with customers. The firework shows made Ryogoku all the more famous. Large, elaborate firework shows were very expensive, but people loved the idea of the enormous expense vanishing in mere seconds and delighted in each explosion. The firework shows stopped during the war and postwar years but were revived in 1978. The show is given on the last Saturday of July at two locations farther upstream. The best way to enjoy the full splendor and excitement of the show is to view it on board a boat floating on the river. Boathouses along the river provide this service.

As you retrace your steps along the main road, you will notice a couple more unique restaurants. One is **Momonjiya** もも

んじや ⑩, which specializes in dishes using the meat of boar, deer, and bear. *(Open 12:00–14:00, 17:00–21:00. Closed on the first and third Sundays during April, May, and June.)* Across the street from Momonjiya is **Kikyoya** 桔梗屋 ⑪, which is famous for eel and *dojō*. *(Open 11:00-14:00, 16:30-21:00. Closed on Sundays and holidays.)* Back at the Ryogoku 1-chome intersection, your direction is straight on, but if you turn left, there is a good *chanko nabe* restaurant, **Kawasaki** 川崎 ⑫, marked by a black signboard with a large sumo wrestler's face. In accordance with the traditional recipe, they use only chicken meat because "being on four legs" means defeat in sumo. *(Open 17:00–22:00. Closed on Sundays and national holidays. For reservations, call 3631-2529.)*

Continuing straight along the main road, you will find the arched gate of **Ekoin** 回向院 ⑬ on the right. Close to the end of the approach to the modern main building is a huge stone monument commemorating the mighty power of sumo wrestlers. Part of the hair cut when a famous wrestler retires is buried underneath the stone. Around a group of old stone bas-reliefs to the left, a few concrete charnels stand surrounded by stacks of *sotoba* sticks. These are bone depositories for dead pets, and the numerous wooden sticks have been left in memory.

Ekoin was first dedicated to the victims of the great fire of 1657, but later it became a prayer temple for the repose of any unidentified dead person or even animal. Some of the old stone monuments are memorials given to the victims of shipwrecks and earthquakes. Some are tombs of Edo-period writers. Their varied designs are extremely interesting. Behind a simple roofed altar is the tomb of a half-legendary robber called Nezumi Kozo (Rat Boy), who died in 1831. He stole from the wealthy and distributed the money to the hard-pressed poor. His great agility gave rise to his nickname. A small chip of stone from his tomb was, and still is, believed to bring good luck in risky pursuits such as gambling, and many people come for a lucky chip. To prevent the disintegration of the tombstone, which has been replaced many times, a couple of stones for chipping are placed in front. Nowadays, most chippers are students who wish for good luck in their school entrance exams.

Since the 1780s sumo tournaments have been special annual events at this temple. The Edo-period tournaments were held in a makeshift hut, but in the early twentieth century a magnificent domed-roof building was built specifically for professional matches. The building, designed by Dr. Kingo Tatsuno, was a precious landmark of early Meiji-period Western architecture, but has since been demolished. Leaving Ekoin, cross the street and walk straight to Ryogoku Station. You may end your walk here, but if you wish to continue, go under the railway overpass.

On your right is the **Kokugikan Sumo Arena** 国技館 ⑭, built in 1984 on the site of the former switchyard of Ryogoku Station. The Kokugikan boasts a capacity of 11,500 and has a ring which can be mechanically removed when not in use for sumo so that various other sports and non-sports events can be held there. Particularly interesting are its special emergency provisions, reflecting the area's long history of natural and man-made disasters. Underneath the stairway between the first and second floors are rooms for food storage, and in part of the second level of the basement is a 3,000-ton water tank for recycling rainwater. A small museum on the first floor is open for public viewing on weekdays free of charge. *(9:30–16:30. Paid audience only during a tournament session.)* The display includes wood-block prints, scroll paintings, wrestlers' aprons, and other items.

From the Kokugikan, continue straight on. Your next destination is a garden near the green-domed building of the Sumida Ward Public Hall seen ahead. If you like curry, **Half Mint** ハーフミント ⑮, on the other side of the street, serves spicy curry with rice or *nan* bread. *(Open 11:00–22:00. Closed on Mondays.)* Next to it is the station for boat cruising down the Sumida River. The trips include a long upstream course and a shorter downstream course to Kasai Seaside Park. *(Tickets are* *available upon reservation by calling 5608-8869, 9:00-17:00 every day except December 29 through January 3.)*

A walled-in area just before the domed building is the **Yasuda Garden** 安田庭園 ⑯. The back entrance is usually closed—to reach the front gate turn right. In the distance ahead, the **Edo-Tokyo Museum** 江戸東京博物館 ⑰ looms large in a very unusual design, looking like a gigantic ice-skate. For now, however, turn left and follow the bend in the road. Soon you will come to the entrance of the Yasuda Garden at the crossroads with traffic lights.

This garden was built by a daimyo during the Edo period and has a tidal pond in the center. It is the only remaining tidal pond still functioning, although the adjustment of the water level is now done artificially and not by the ebb and flow of the Sumida River. The garden changed hands after the Meiji Restoration and became the property of Zenjiro Yasuda, the head of the Yasuda Zaibatsu, who gave it to the city of Tokyo upon his death. In 1923, when the Great Earthquake hit this area, the garden was almost completely destroyed, but has subsequently been restored to its original beauty by the Sumida Ward Office.

The path winds through the garden and eventually brings you back to the entrance gate. Leave the garden and cross over to a woody park, **Yokoamicho Koen** 横網町公園 ⑲. You are entering the park from its back gate, and as you walk, you can view the castle-like back of the Cenotaph Hall, built in memory of the victims of the Great Earthquake. After World War II, the hall also served as a place to remember the dead from the Tokyo air raids.

The site of this park, along with several other neighboring blocks, used to belong to a military-clothing factory. In 1922 the land was given to the city of Tokyo to be used as a public park and schools. Before construction started, however, the area was struck by the Great Earthquake. Tens of thousands of people crammed into this open space, which was bare of trees and buildings. Their relief lasted for only a couple of hours, however, as flames all around heated the air, turning it into a burning tornado, which took their lives.

Flames enveloped this area again in 1945 from midnight of March 9 until the next morning. This time it was caused by low-flying American aircraft showering nearly 2,000 tons of M69 napalm bombs over heavily populated Shitamachi. The military operation took a heavy toll of 77,000 lives overnight. During the two years of 1944 and 1945 more than 100,000 Tokyoites lost their lives from intensive bombing. This number is comparable to the number of victims from the atomic bombing of Hiroshima. Every year on March 10, a special service is held at the Cenotaph Hall to pray for the repose of the souls of the victims and for world peace.

You may walk into the Cenotaph Hall through an entrance in the front. On the walls are oil paintings depicting the Great Earthquake, works by an artist who made many sketches of the disaster immediately after. The interior design is a unique combination of a Christian chapel and a Buddhist altar, and the exterior stairways resemble those of a Shinto shrine. As you leave the park from its front gate, look back at the overall design of the hall, which is based on the image of a bird about to fly up with spread wings. The architect was Dr. Chuta Ito, who also designed the Hongan-ji temple in Tsukiji and Meiji-jingu shrine in Harajuku.

Leaving the park, turn left. At the traffic light, cross the street and turn left toward a large bridge. The bridge and the area beyond it are called Kuramae, which means "in front of the *kura*" (storehouses). They are so named because of the presence of many rice granaries here during the Edo period. These granaries were used for storing rice collected from the shogun's own estates until its seasonal distribution to the shogun's retainers.

Unlike the high-ranking daimyo, who were based in fiefs outside Edo, the lesser vassals received their stipends in rice, which was their only official source of income. Part of the rice was sold for cash in order to buy other daily necessities. The paying-out of rice at the granaries in Kuramae caused a tremendous rush of carts and carriers sent by the 20,000 retainers. Some of them, not caring for the rush and long waiting lines, asked men of the small refreshment stands in this area to be their agents. By around 1729 these Kuramae rice agents had set themselves up in business. They were called *fudasashi* because they made a practice of thrusting *(sasu)* sticks with the clients' name plates *(fuda)* into the rice bales under their keeping. The job soon proved to be an extremely profitable business because they also monopolized rice sales and even loans against rice to be received. They charged high interest rates, over 20 percent, or even 100 percent in some extreme cases. The majority of samurai in peace time had no other recourse but to sell their rations to these loan sharks.

WEST BANK COURSE   Cross the bridge. The large nine-story building seen on the left of the road is the Tokyo Regional Bureau of Postal Savings. Walk past it, and you will arrive at the Kuramae 1-chome intersection, with a firework shop called **Yamagata Shoten** 山形商店 ⑲ on the right. Several blocks to the right of the intersection is the so-called Kuramae toy wholesalers district. Kuramae Station on the Toei Asakusa Line is nearby. From track 1, you can take a train bound for Nihombashi. To the left of the intersection is the Asakusabashi shopping center for dolls and shop displays. A short detour straight ahead is suggested for a visit to **Torigoe-jinja** 鳥越神社 ⑳. The shrine is located at the second light from the intersection. Although its compound has been substantially reduced, it is one of the oldest shrines in Tokyo. Its summer festival, on a weekend around June 7 every year, is very active and known for its day-long parade of the shrine's heavy *omikoshi*. By the time the portable shrine has returned from its tour of all the towns in the parish, dusk has fallen; as numerous lighted lanterns swing, you can hear the melancholic echo of *kiyari* songs. Another interesting festival is Donto, held on January 9, which has evolved from the ancient farmers' prayers for good harvest in the coming year. This rural festival is called Koshogatsu, the lesser New Year, now rarely seen in modern Tokyo. Pine and straw decorations used for New Year are burned in the shrine compound. Rice cakes are baked in this fire and then eaten, supposedly to protect against disease during the coming year. *(The ritual bonfire takes place around 13:00. For confirmation, call 3851-5033.)*

Backtracking to the Kuramae 1-chome intersection, turn right to explore the colorful pell-mell of interior decorations, kitchen accessories, and packaging materials. At the JR Asakusabashi Station, you can take a train home.

If you have some time left, cross the street in front of the station. There are two large doll shops, **Shugetsu** 秀月 ㉑ and **Kyugetsu** 久月 ㉒ , both long-established in this business. If you are hungry, a short detour further to the left will take you to a wonderful *yakitori* restaurant, **Toriyasu** 鳥安 ㉓ . Past the traffic light with Mitsubishi Bank on the corner, take the second right. A white four-story building on the left embraces an old-fashioned tavern inside. A red-and-black paper lantern hung from the eaves indicates the entrance. Inside, worn beams and a counter of smoked wood have successfully recreated the warm atmosphere of a cozy restaurant-bar. The lunch time special is *kiji-jū* (slices of grilled chicken on rice) with miso soup and a small salad on the side. *(Open 11:30-13:15, 16:30-22:00. Closed on the first Sunday. Tel: 3851-6366.)*

Backtrack toward the JR station, and just before the railway overpass, turn left to visit a thriving *washi* paper-crafts shop, **Sakura Horikiri** さくらほりきり ㉔ , in the fourth block on the left, with its entrance marked by a blue awning. On the first and second floors, colorful *washi* is sold at about 20 percent less than elsewhere, along with many kits to make boxes, dolls, and framed pictures. Classes are given regularly. *(For information, call 3864-1773.)*

Leaving the paper shop, turn right and take the second arch to go under the railway overpass. A modern white building immediately on the left hides a secret cave stocked with antiques, it is actually a coffee shop called **Kahido** 可否道 ㉕. A humorous pottery badger awaits visitors at the door, which slides open to reveal a dimly lit interior decorated with miscellaneous antiques and rows of beautiful teacups. The coffee brewed from choice beans is expensive, but such moments of relaxation make you forget the busy world outside.

Near Kahido, several buildings further down along the same street on the right, is **Hyakumangoku** 百万石 ㉖ , a good *tonkatsu* restaurant. *(Closed on Sundays, holidays, and the third Saturday.)* Still continuing straight to the end of the road, turn left to visit a green bridge called Yanagibashi. Several huts projecting over the water provide boats for fishing and party cruises. **Komatsuya** 小松屋, closest to the bridge, is recommended for its authentic service. *(Tel: 3851-2780.)*

This area, also called Yanagibashi after the bridge, prospered as a pleasure district. Taking a boat from here to the Yoshiwara was popular with upper-class dandies. Many high-class restaurants thrived, and the streets were frequented by chic women and customers. One of the most famous restaurants, **Kameseiro** 亀清楼 ㉗, continues in business in the brown building by the bridge. Try their exquisite cuisine offered as *obentō* in a lacquered box. *(Miyakodori bentō is suggested. For a large group, a beautiful tatami-matted room overlooking the Sumida River is available upon reservation. Tel: 3851-3101. Open 11:30-14:00, 17:00-21:00. Closed on Sundays and holidays.)*

As you stand at the green bridge and look toward the Sumida River, the Ryogoku bridge can be seen in the distance. Further beyond is Fukagawa, with which Yanagibashi competed for prosperity. Both areas benefitted from the generous patronage of wealthy commoners; its women entertainers and their patrons took pride in their sophisticated taste in fashion and art which emphasized simplicity and subdued colors, different from the more flamboyant fashions of western Japan. Their taste was termed *iki*, and represents the peak of the urban sophistication reached by the inhabitants of Edo.

Retrace your steps along the Kanda River and keep walking

straight until you come to yet another bridge, Asakusabashi. During the Edo period, this bridge served as an important checkpoint for boats sailing upstream the Kanda River to reach the city center. Inspection was made of pedestrians, too, who traveled along the main road here to the Asakusa Kannon temple and farther beyond to Nikko and northern Japan. A stone monument is erected on the other side of the bridge in memory of this checkpoint. Cross the street and turn right to return to Asakusabashi Station, visiting **Yoshitoku** 吉徳 ㉘, another famous doll shop with a long history, on the way.

Otsukaresama.
(Well done! You must be tired.)

FUKAGAWA

Walking time
Monzen Nakacho–Kiyosumi Garden: 1 hour
Kiyosumi Garden–Morishita: 1 hour 30 minutes

BACKGROUND   Fukagawa was a prosperous lumber district in the seventeenth and eighteenth centuries. Its proximity to the sea also led to its development as a shipping center for rice, salt, and fertilizer. It was a very masculine society, the tone being set by the numerous sailors and longshoremen who were drawn by the profits that could be made from risky shipping ventures.

In the Meiji era, the riverside was host to many factories; cement and textiles were among this area's major products. After the end of World War II, however, environmental concerns drove many of the factories out, and their spacious lots have been redeveloped into office buildings and condominiums. Local residents, regretting the demise of traditional customs, have been endeavoring to preserve what remains of the old lifestyles. The Fukagawa Edo Museum, the highlight of this course, is one successful example of such endeavors. Life-size reproductions of late Edo-period buildings vividly convey the cozy atmosphere of the common people's town. Close to the museum, Kiyosumi Garden shows the spacious luxury enjoyed by a Meiji-era plutocrat. The summer festival of Tomioka Hachiman and the tour of the seven lucky gods at New Year are good occasions to get a feel for this area's lively atmosphere.

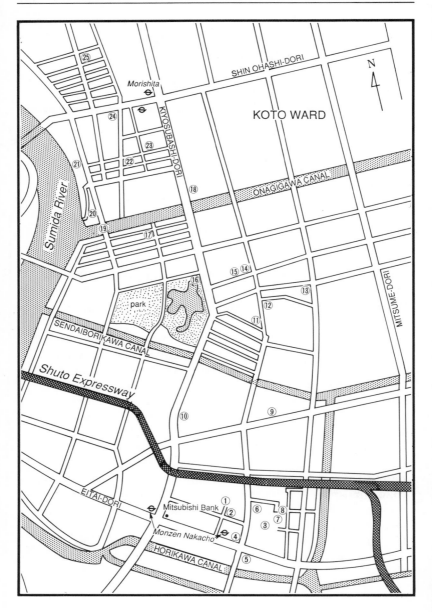

GETTING THERE   Take the Tozai Line to Monzen Nakacho Station. Exit the subway station by using the stairway closest to Kiba, the next station, which will be at the front of your train if you are traveling from central Tokyo. Once past the ticket gate, turn left and ascend the steps to the street.

Immediately outside the subway exit is the red-painted gate of **Fukagawa Fudo** 深川不動 temple ①. An approach to the right leads to the main building. On the days of its *ennichi*, which are the 1, 15, and 28 of every month, the approach and nearby streets are lined with stalls. Immediately on the right of the approach is a shop selling tasty *ageman* (deep-fried dumplings with sweet bean-paste in the center). Across the street is an ivory shop with a bronze elephant in front. Past some more shops, you will come to a crossroads with an old-looking temple called **Eitai-ji** 永代寺 ② on the right.

After viewing Eitai-ji, walk to the end of the approach to the green-roofed building of Fukagawa Fudo. Often, powerful sutra chanting can be heard from a loudspeaker even before reaching the main building. Notice an elaborately crafted bronze incense burner on a high stand at the top of the steps and a roofed fountain to its left, where purifying water flows out of a pair of delightful cast-metal dragons. These, along with the statues of child guardians, are donations by ardent worshipers. At the shop nearby, talismans and amulets are sold. The numerous small wooden sticks are called *gomagi* and are offerings to Fudo, enshrined in the main building. They are placed in boxes according to the kind of request. After writing your name, age, and address on the sticks, they are left at the counter with a monetary offering, and are later burned in a ritual performed by the temple's abbot to consecrate the wishes. This *goma* ritual is an important service in esoteric Buddhism.

Fudo is highly revered in esoteric Buddhism. Originally worshiped by the Jains in ancient India, Fudo is conceived as a god of justice, who fends off evil spirits with his sword and menacing look, thus helping his worshipers accomplish their wishes. He is usually depicted with a halo of flames behind him or wrapped in a glowing fire. In popular belief, the god needs to constantly replenish his power with the blazing energy of fire; thus a sign on the counter reads, "These *gomagi* sticks are the food of the Fudo god." The *goma* fire service is conducted several times a day on the 1, 15, and 28 of each month to powerful drum beats and resonant incantations. Walk back to the red gate and turn left to pass by two blocks of shops and restaurants before you come to **Tomioka Hachiman** 富岡八幡 ③.

The area on the other side of this main street is the once famous Fukagawa red-light district, now mostly drinking houses and traditional restaurants. The night spots in Fukagawa originated as tea houses licensed in 1655 by the shogunate to provide food for visitors to the Hachiman shrine. The restaurants soon began catering to visitors' erotic appetites as well, competing with the Yoshiwara district. Female geisha first appeared in Fukagawa around the year 1750 as professional entertainers paid for their musical and dancing talents. Earlier, the term "geisha" had been used for men who were accomplished in Noh, Kyogen, Kabuki, music, or other arts. Not so snobbish as the Yoshiwara courtesans, the Fukagawa geisha gained in popularity along with the rising economic power of commoners in the early eighteenth century.

Just before you reach the gigantic torii of Tomioka Hachiman, a little off to the left of the street, you will see **Italian Tomato** ④ on the left-hand corner, which serves reasonably priced lunches. Diagonally across the main street is a good *soba* restaurant, **Hoseian** 宝盛庵 ⑤ . *(Open 11:00–15:00 and 16:00–20:00. Closed on Thursdays.)*

Inside the large torii to your right, you will notice a group of sumo-related stone monuments. Inscribed on a pair of slabs are the names of wrestlers who have attained the second-highest rank of *ōzeki*. The flanking stones show the sizes of the feet, hands, and height of some jumbo wrestlers in the recorded history of sumo since the mid-eighteenth century. The main building of the shrine in red, green, and gold is usually quiet, enveloped by thick foliage. On the days of its annual festival on and around August 15, however, the spacious compound is full of people and stalls. The scale and vigor of this festival competes with that of the Sanja Matsuri in Asakusa in May. In the early nineteenth century, the overheated excitement of the festival caused an accident: the nearby Eitaibashi bridge over the Sumida River collapsed from the weight of the enormous crowd. The people of Edo had been eager to celebrate this festival after a twelve-year ban by the shogunate, and the date of the festival had been postponed for four days due to heavy rain. When the weather cleared on August 19, the people rushed to the shrine from Nihombashi and other parts of the city, pulling decorated floats and carrying *omikoshi*. When they began crossing the bridge, a central support gave way, and hundreds of people in festival costumes were drowned.

Today the shrine holds a full-scale festival every three years, on the weekend closest to August 15. On both days, *omikoshi* are carried through the streets. The highlight is the grand parade of more than fifty *omikoshi*; as the carriers jostle along, wildly tossing the portable shrines, neighbors splash bucketfuls of water over them. In the din of shouts and raucous activity, the stifling heat is forgotten. All the money needed for the festival, amounting to several hundred million yen, is funded by donations from residents. *(To confirm the dates of the next major festival, call 3642-1315.)*

In a thicket near the left-hand balcony of the main building are some smooth round stones commemorating the weight-lifting skills developed during the Edo period by longshoremen working at warehouses on the Sumida River. The winners of the weight-lifting competitions attributed their success to the gods of this shrine, and in appreciation they gave the winning stones as offerings. Their skills became a traditional practice and have been designated an intangible folk asset by the Tokyo Metropolitan Government.

Go down the steps beyond the stones, turn to the right, and you will come to three small shrines. The middle one is dedicated to **Ebisu** 恵比寿 ⑥, one of the gods on the seven lucky gods tour in the Fukagawa area. Return to the front of the main building and go around to the other side, passing under a bridge which connects two buildings. On the right are more **stone monuments** 横綱記念碑 ⑦, given to all the *yokozuna*, the highest-ranking sumo wrestlers. A pair of massive flat stones in front depict a famous match in 1875 at Ekoin. On the middle slab are engraved the names of the generations of *yokozuna* up to the forty-fifth, and on two more stones on both sides, the other wrestlers' names include current ones.

To the right of these stones, you will see an Inari shrine, surrounded by red-painted wooden railings, and a small pond beyond them. Across the pond is a tiny shrine on the left and a path leading away from it towards a small torii; pass through it and you will see a larger torii on the left. Pass through the large torii and turn left at the next crossing. The charming, simple truss bridge is called **Hachimanbashi** 八幡橋 ⑧. The bridge was built in 1878, originally at a location on the other side of the Sumida River, close to Nihombashi. It was designed by an American engineer, Squire Whipple.

The road beyond the bridge bends to the right. Take the first left and walk straight until the road meets a major street, where you turn right. Walk straight, passing under the Shuto Expressway. At a major intersection with a gas station on the right, cross the street and turn right. Past several buildings from the corner stands **Fuyuki Benten** 冬木弁天 ⑨, the second of the seven lucky gods in this area. Fuyuki Benten used to be a private shrine of the Fuyuki family, who were successful lumber merchants in this area dating back to 1705. Until the Great Earthquake of 1923, they owned an extensive tract of land here and the family's name now identifies the area.

The lumber business in Fukagawa started after the Great Fire of 1657, when the shogunate hastened to reclaim Fukagawa from a vast swampland to relocate lumber merchants from the Nihombashi area. The lumber men were invited soon after Ieyasu became the shogun and started building Edo Castle. In the construction boom which followed, the lumber business grew by leaps and bounds. However, the mountains of lumber at the original stockyards close to Nihombashi burned fast during the Great Fire and exacerbated the damage. Thus, moving them away from the city center became a priority in the reconstruction of Edo, and Fukagawa on the other side of the Sumida River was chosen as the new site.

Return to the intersection and turn right. However, if you are interested in visiting **Shingyo-ji** 心行寺 ⑩ , related to the third of the lucky gods, Fukurokuju, walk straight to the next traffic light and turn right. The lucky god is enshrined in a hexagonal building to the left of the temple's main building. Otherwise, turn right at the traffic light nearest to Fuyuki Benten. Walk straight and cross a bridge over a canal flowing into the Sumida River on the left. From here the seventeenth-century haiku poet Matsuo Basho sailed out for his famous trip to northern Japan, recorded in *The Narrow Path to the Deep North*. At the next traffic light, cross the intersection toward **Enjuin** 円珠院 ⑪ on the left of the street, which is related to Daikoku, the fourth of the seven lucky gods. A charming stone statue of this god stands to the left of a modern building with an altar in the left-hand section.

Continuing straight along the walls of the graveyards on both sides of the main street, you will pass by a small restaurant, **Ayame** あやめ ⑫ , with a blue *noren* with an iris logo. It serves home-cooked-style tempura which comes in a lacquered box with a big bowl of miso soup and a small salad. *(The tempura lunch is called tenjū. Closed on Wednesdays.)*

Walk to the next intersection with a traffic light, turn right and walk to the next traffic light. On this corner is **Ryukoin** 竜光院 ⑬ , related to the god Bishamon, another of the seven lucky gods. You will be passing by home- and workshop-type small businesses dealing in furniture, house painting, or box making. Turn left at the corner of Ryukoin and left at the next traffic light. Several blocks and a traffic light away, a three-story grayish-white building on the right is the **Fukagawa Edo Folk Museum** 深川江戸資料館 ⑭, opened in November 1986. It houses marvelous reproductions of old buildings. The architects and designers together have done wonders in recreating an Edo-period Shitamachi town. An excellent English brochure is available in a unique first-person narrative style. *(Open 10:00–17:00 throughout most of the year except the yearend and New Year period and two unspecified days for annual checkup. Tel: 3630-8625)*

If you wish to go straight to this museum from the Monzen Nakacho subway station, take Exit 3. Coming out on the street, turn left and walk underneath the Shuto Expressway. Cross the main street, Kiyosumi-dori, at some point and keep straight for about fifteen minutes. Look for white banners and a pair of dark brown lanterns indicating the approach to the museum on the right.

From the entrance, go left past numerous panels depicting craftsmen, street hawkers, travelling musicians, and so on, against a backdrop copied from an old screen painting. You come out to a landing overlooking the recreated old town. Descending the stairway to the basement, you plunge at once into an astonishingly real Fukagawa as it was about two hundred years ago. Everything from houses and a fire lookout tower, to Edo-period vegetables sold at the grocer, are reproduced. Computerized lighting and sound effects enhance the atmosphere of a lively riverside town. There are also videotape displays showing documentary films on contemporary traditional craftsmen in Koto Ward, as well as a recreation hall and a theater with a capacity of three hundred. *(For information call 3630-8625.)*

Adjacent to the museum is a stately temple called **Reigan-ji** 霊巌寺 ⑮. As you enter its gate, your attention will be drawn to the majestic main building and a nine-foot-high bronze Jizo to its left. At the back of the compound there are more Jizo in a group of six, three of which date from the early Edo period and retain a naive pastoral charm.

This Jizo is one of the Six Jizo of Edo, erected by the priest Shogen between 1708 and 1720, and patterned after the Six Jizo of Kyoto. In appreciation for his recovery from a serious disease, Shogen dedicated his time and energy to placing six magnificent bronze statues of Jizo at locations along the city border, including Asakusa, Shinagawa, Shinjuku, Toshima, and Fukagawa.

Jizo is a Buddhist bodhisattva who has been revered since the tenth century as a savior from all kinds of sufferings. He usually takes the form of a priest with a ball in his left hand and a staff in the right. Based on a belief that Jizo can appear in all six worlds of Buddhist cosmology—the worlds of hell, hungry spirits, animals, fighting spirits, human beings, and heaven—statues are often erected in groups of six. Jizo is also believed to have special compassion for children who have died and wander on the graveled shore of the river separating this world from the others. Because of this belief, piles of pebbles are placed in front of Jizo statues, and bibs and other things usually associated with young children are offered.

Leave Reigan-ji and turn right. At the major street, Kiyosumi-dori, cross over toward the walled-in woods of **Kiyosumi Garden** 清澄庭園 ⑩ ahead. Turn right and take the next left to come to the entrance of the garden at a crossroads. To enter, pay a small fee. You may walk freely through the garden, but you must exit through the entrance gate. The elegant traditional house projecting over the water of the pond is a reproduction of a special lodge built to entertain British General H.H. Kitchener when he visited Japan in 1909. Both this house and another house by the gate can be rented for a fee. *(For information, call 3641-5892.)* If you wish to finish your tour here, you may go back to Monzen Nakacho by going back to the Kiyosumi-dori and turning right. Walk straight to the subway station.

To continue the course, however, take a small street which leads straight away from the garden's gate to the north. Cross a major street and stop at a small shrine standing at the second crossing. This is **Fukagawa Inari** 深川稲荷 ⑰, related to the god Hotei of the seven lucky gods. Your direction is to the left, but you might be interested in a detour to a famous *dojō* restaurant near here. Turn right at Fukagawa Inari. You will come back to the Kiyosumi-dori, where you turn left. Go over a bridge and cross the street to come to **Iseki** 伊せ喜⑱, housed in a graceful traditional building. Its entrance is marked by a blue *noren* with the three *hiragana* symbols, *do-ze-u* どぜう. It would be fun to try either delicious *yanagawa* (fillets of *dojō* cooked with vegetables and eggs), or *nukinabe* (deboned *dojō* cooked at your table). Rice, soup, and other things have to be ordered separately. *(Open 11:30-14:00, 16:00-20:30. Closed on Mondays.)*

Going left from Fukagawa Inari, take the second right to come to **Mannenbashi** 万年橋 ⑲, a steel bow-string girder bridge painted light blue. The seventeenth-century wooden original was loved by Edo-period artists for its grand view of the Sumida River with Mt. Fuji in the distance. Both Hiroshige and Hokusai depicted this bridge in bold designs. Unfortunately, highrises now block the once-famous sight.

The Haiku poet Basho lived in this neighborhood on and off for more than ten years. Although the exact location cannot be determined, an Inari shrine, named **Basho Inari** 芭蕉稲荷 ⑳, has been erected in a small street to the left beyond the bridge. Returning to the main street, turn left and walk straight past a traffic light, where you will find a modern three-story white building with a traditional garden gate made of bamboo and twigs. This is the **Basho Memorial Hall** 芭蕉記念館 ㉑, built in 1981. Pay a nominal admission fee at the entrance, and you can view a collection of materials related to Basho, including haiku written in his own calligraphy and paintings and poems by his followers. Two tastefully designed tatami-matted rooms over-looking the Sumida River are available for rent at a nominal fee. *(For information, call 3631-1448. Closed on Mondays and at the yearend and New Year period.)*

Leaving the museum, cross the street and bear right. In the fourth block on the right, a restaurant called **Miyako** みや古 ㉒ offers a rice dish named *Fukagawa-meshi* with a bowl of soup and cooked vegetables on the side. The soy-sauce-flavored steamed rice mixed with *asari* (clams) is a revival of prewar Fukagawa home cooking. *(Open 11:30–14:00 and 17:00–21:00.)* Continuing straight, however, a gray concrete torii on the left marks the entrance to **Fukagawa Shimmei-gu** 深川神明宮 ㉓, related to Jurojin, the last of the seven lucky gods. Storehouses for portable shrines flank the approach. Beyond the storage building on the right are two shrines, one dedicated to Inari and the other dedicated to Jurojin. The main building with its green roof and *chigi* (crossed gables) is simple and beautiful.

Fukagawa Shimmei-gu is the oldest religious establishment in Koto-ku. It was founded by Fukagawa Hachiroemon, who came here from Osaka with his followers about 450 years ago. His hard work was acknowledged by Ieyasu, who said the area should be named after him. Further south, land reclamation continues by filling in the sea with the waste matter of Tokyo's thirteen million people. The summer festival of this shrine is less well known than Tomioka Hachiman's, but is equally boisterous. It begins in the evening of August 15, followed by the procession of a jumbo *omikoshi* on the 16, and on the 17, a parade of community portable shrines.

Leaving the shrine, turn left and left again at the main street, Kiyosumi-dori. To the left of the second traffic light is the entrance to the Morishita subway station on the Toei Shinjuku Line. From track 1, you can take a train either straight to Shinjuku or to Ogawamachi, where you can transfer to the Chiyoda or Marunouchi lines. If you have time, walk a couple more blocks past the subway entrance and a traffic light to visit **Rengatei** 煉瓦亭 ㉔, a branch of a reputable Western-style restaurant in Ginza. *(Closed on Wednesdays.)* The Sumida River is nearby, and across the Shin Ohashi bridge, the Ginza and

Marunouchi, Tokyo's prime business section, are only two miles southwest.

This neighborhood is attracting special attention recently, not just because of its promixity to the heart of Tokyo, but for a successful redevelopment of an old dye works into rehearsal studios for stage shows and a unique theater, **Benisan Studios** and **Benisan Pit** ベニサンスタジオ and ベニサンピット ㉕. To visit them, cross the street in front of Rengatei. Walk straight and turn left at the first traffic light. Beige brick buildings on the right used to churn out colorful fabrics and yarn, but now produce top-class dramas and musicals. Ennosuke's *Yamato Takeru*, Ninagawa's *Oedipus*, and a fashion show by Kansai have been rehearsed here.

In the late 1970s, when stricter ecological regulations caused the production facilities to move out of Tokyo, Benisan Company could easily have sold the land to any of the developers avidly seeking a large site close to central Tokyo. The whole neighborhood could also easily have been engulfed in a surge of highrise construction projects. What prompted the company's management to opt for preservation and use of their historic buildings for a creative purpose was basically the Shitamachi love of community. In 1983 they conceived the idea of providing a low-cost rehearsal place for drama companies and thus attract people from other areas. The plan entailed large investments for refurbishing machine rooms and storage space. You can get a glimpse of the creative activities inside by visiting an attached cafe-bar on other side of the block, accessible through the two Benisan buildings. Called Pit-In, it is up two flights of steel stairway. *(Open 11:30–22:30. Closed on Tuesdays.)* In a chic lounge and bar they serve good coffee and simple dishes such as spaghetti and fried rice. From the other door of the lounge, you can take a quick look at Benisan Pit Theater, which is beyond a door immediately on the right. To return, walk back the same way to the subway station.

*   *   *

SUGGESTED DETOUR   A family of silk dyers specializing in

sarasa-zome (Japanese-style batik using stencil-dye techniques) to make material for women's kimono, live close to Ojima Station (four stops on the Toei Shinjuku Line). At Ojima Station, take Exit A6 and turn left, and left again at the traffic light. Walking through a lively shopping center along a curving road, you will come to a small crossing with a relatively large greengrocer on the right and a *nori* (seaweed) shop on the left. Go left along a narrow road to find **Sara Hama** さら浜 silk dyers on the right, operated by the Sano family. Stepping into their workshop, you might be surprised by the exquisitely beautiful hand-printed silk materials produced in seemingly poor working conditions. About a dozen long wooden boards are set on low stands on a mud floor, looking like low benches. Several men—the senior Sano over eighty years old, his two sons, and a helper—stand stooping over the boards, intent on rubbing in the dye, using finely-cut paper stencils. They overlay slightly different patterns in twenty or more steps, changing the color each time. All the tools and techniques used, including their postures, are the results of long, diligent effort.

Sarasa-zome was developed in the late Edo period, combining the traditional technique of stencil print and the exotic floral designs of imported batik. Dye-resistant rice paste is used to leave spots undyed, unlike Javanese batik which uses wax. After the printing, the fabric is steamed to set the dyes, rinsed, and stretch-dried. The multicolored decorative materials were in great fashion until prewar years. Recent dwindling demand due to decreased use of kimono in daily life has prompted the Sanos to adapt their excellent skills to custom-print cotton materials for boutiques or T-shirts and handkerchiefs. Small items using their fine materials, such as bags and table mats, are often available for sale.

> *Shitamachi no hito wa shinsetsu desu*
> (People of Shitamachi are kind.)

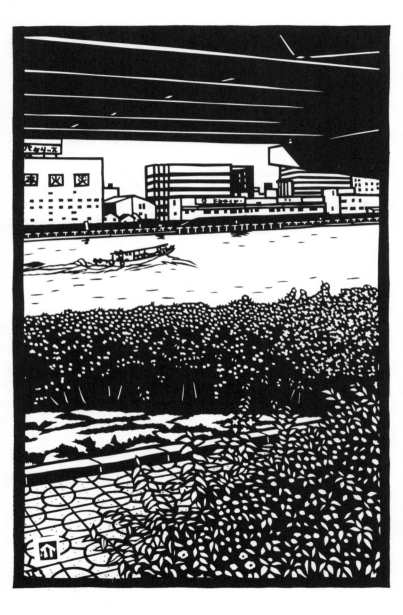

MUKOJIMA

Walking time
3 hours

BACKGROUND   This course along the east bank of the
Sumida River is especially popular during the first week of the
New Year when Tokyoites visit temples and shrines related to
the *shichifukujin* (seven gods of good luck). Each temple or
shrine sells a miniature representing its particular god. A complete set includes the seven gods together with a small boat on
which to place them. When taken home and displayed, this or-
nament is said to bring good luck throughout the year.

Faith in the *shichifukujin* probably dates back to medieval
times when merchants worshiped a god supposed to bring
business prosperity. Faith in other gods of good luck spread,
and gradually they were grouped together during the Edo period. The seven gods are a hodgepodge of gods originating in
India, China, and Japan, and each is associated with a moral or
personal virtue, such as popularity, longevity, charm, integrity, influence, wealth, and generosity. A round trip to the
seven temples and shrines of these gods during the first few
days of January was a popular practice among the Edo townspeople, and it still is in Shitamachi today.

GETTING THERE   Take the Ginza Line to Asakusa and ascend the stairway in the middle of the platform. After passing
through the ticket gate, turn left and climb the stairs leading to

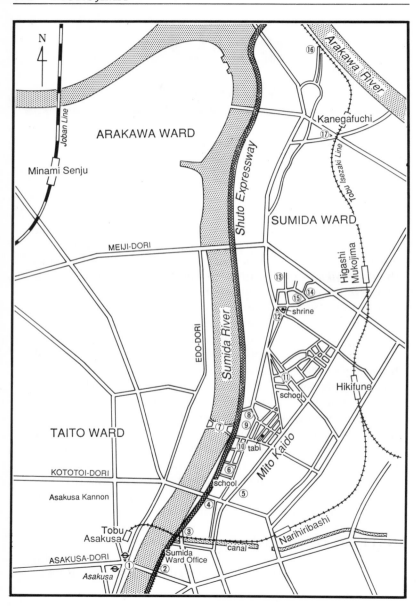

Exit 4 to come out at Azumabashi, a large bridge spanning the Sumida River. The Mukojima area lies on the other side of the river to the left.

Straight ahead of the subway exit is a boathouse, **Amisei** あ み清 ① , providing cruising and fishing services. A party cruise by *yakatabune* (traditional boat) was formerly a pleasure which only the privileged could afford. This custom had nearly died out but has now been revived, complete with karaoke singing. *(For information about chartering a boat, call Amisei at 3844-1869.)* As you cross the bridge, notice an enormous gilded object decorating the top of the **Asahi Beer Hall** アサヒビアホール②.

As part of a large-scale redevelopment of this area, the bank of the river, which used to be a drab concrete wall, has been refurbished into an attractive walkway. After crossing the bridge, take a small stairway immediately on the left to walk along the promenade. At the end of the pavement, ascend a small graveled stairway and bear left at the top. At the traffic light, cross over to the other side of the road and turn left to cross a bridge with many *yakatabune* floating on the water underneath. On the right is a park, **Sumida Koen** 隅田公園 ③. Take the path a short distance ahead to enter, and turn left past a small open space for a stroll between low hills on the right and a beautiful pond on the left.

This park was formerly the suburban residence of Lord Tokugawa of Mito, one of the three branch families of the Tokugawa family in the feudal age. The Great Kanto Earthquake of 1923 destroyed the highly celebrated garden, which had been visited by the Emperor and Empress Meiji. In 1931, the whole compound was designated a public park, and many efforts have since been made to restore the garden's original splendor. The park is now a well-maintained oasis for neighbors and visitors to enjoy cherry blossoms in the spring and iris in early summer. The park merges with the quiet precincts of a relatively large shrine, **Ushijima-jinja** 牛島神社 ④ , dedicated to the tutelary god of this area. Inside the dim main building are a huge pair of carved lionheads. To the right as you face the main building is a black stone cow called the "caressing cow," presented to the shrine in 1824. It was believed that if you stroked the part of the cow's body corresponding to your own ailing part and prayed for recovery, the cow would work a miracle cure. The smooth shiny texture of the statue gives mute evidence to the sufferings endured by the Edo commoners. A red bib and numerous paper-crane offerings reflect the stone cow's continuing popularity. Exit from the gate on the right as you face the shrine and turn left toward the main street. Your basic direction is straight, but to cross the main street you must take the intersection to your right.

*   *   *

SUGGESTED DETOUR   *Soba* lovers will enjoy trying the nearby restaurant **Kadoman** 角萬 ⑤. Cross the intersection, again to the right, and then turn left. The restaurant, with a small square lantern hung under the roof, is about ten buildings away, near a large white traffic sign. Their *soba* is *al dente* and rich in flavor. Try either *mori* (cold *soba*) or *kamonan* (noodles in hot soup with meat). *(Open 11:30–19:30. Closed on Sundays and national holidays.)* A little before Kadoman, notice the temporary kite shop **Tohenbokuan** 唐変木庵. These small but authentically crafted kites use bold designs and coloring, and convey the dynamic spirit of Edo townspeople. In 1994, the craftsman, Kanno-san, will be opening a permanent shop across the street from Mimeguri-jinja, your next destination.

If you do not take the detour, walk back a few steps to your left, after first crossing the major street, and take the first right. Past a school on the left is **Mimeguri-jinja** 三囲神社 ⑥, the first shrine on this area's lucky gods tour. Rather exceptionally, this shrine has two pairs of stone guardian animals, dogs and foxes. The dogs are very charming, with curls engraved on their bodies and tails. The sleek foxes are installed closer to the building because they are messengers of the shrine's principal deity, Inari.

Notice a large natural stone placed between the dog and fox on the right-hand side. On it is inscribed a haiku composed in 1693 by Takarai Kikaku. It is said that because the area suffered a drought that year, the farmers got together in the shrine to pray for rain. The poet, who happened to pass by and hear them, composed this poem appealing to the god of rice paddies. To the great joy of the people, the wish was granted, and the next day brought pouring rain which soaked the dry, cracked fields. Behind the shrine on the right is a tunnel of red torii at the end of which are two small shrines. These are dedicated to a legendary fox which used to live here. One shrine is guarded by several perky stone foxes. The old statues in front of the shrines, representing an old man and woman, are sorcerers who could communicate with the fox to convey people's wishes. The inscriptions on the statues date back to 1701. Back at the main shrine, on the left as you face it, is another small shrine in which are enshrined the gods Daikoku and Ebisu, two of the seven lucky gods.

In India, Daikoku was originally a militant god whose mission was to protect Buddhism. The Chinese, however, made him into the guardian of the kitchen and when the god was introduced to Japan, he was associated with the rice harvest, and therefore wealth. This god is usually depicted standing or seated on rice bales, holding a mallet with which he can shake out gold coins and other treasures. Ebisu is a native god who was worshiped by fishermen throughout Japan. The faith spread to the merchant class in the middle ages when Ebisu became the god of business prosperity. He is represented in an ancient courtier's garment, holding a sea bream or a basket in his left hand and a fishing rod in his right. Miniatures of the gods, less than an inch in height, are sold at the shrine's office, to the right as you face the main building. Ask for *gobuntai,* which means "shared scared body." The boat is called *takarabune* or treasure boat.

The next two temples are five minutes' walk to the left from the front gate of this shrine. However, try a short detour along the bank of the Sumida River, which runs behind the shrine. There is a back gate to the riverside, but if it is closed, take the small road to your right between the shrine and the school. Cross the road under the Shuto Expressway and walk up to a promenade on the riverbank, where you turn right.

Lined with rows of cherry trees, the attractive sidewalk is the result of attempts to refurbish the banks of the river after damage done by the construction boom in the 1960s and 1970s. From about the middle of the Edo period, this area was an elegant place to live in or to visit. The cherry trees along the Sumida River became famous all over the country for their fabled beauty depicted in old songs and stories. Poets in particular praised the gorgeous rows of cherry trees showering pink petals over the boats sailing up and down the river. Since then, the concrete embankment and hissing traffic have done little to enhance the elegance of the area. Regretting the lost nature, many groups of people have been working hard to restore the cherry borders and to keep the river clean. The yellow-colored bridge ahead is part of such efforts. Called **Sakurabashi** 桜橋 ⑦ , it is designed in a unique **X** shape for pedestrians only. The bridge and refurbished banks with stairways and benches have attracted people, and this success has led to other similar redevelopments along the river, including the paved walkway at the beginning of today's tour.

Immediately beyond Sakurabashi is a pedestrian bridge tucked underneath the expressway. Though unattractive, it provides a better means of crossing the busy road than the street-level crossing ahead. The steep roof seen on the right as you descend the bridge is one of your destinations, but you will have to detour in order to get to its front. At street level, keep going straight and then turn right.

As you round the curve, on your right is a tall monument surrounded by bushes which tells of the history of the cherry trees along the Sumida River. According to the text, the cherry trees were planted by the eighth shogun, Yoshimune, in the eighteenth century to encourage greenery. Continue straight from the stone monument, turn right, and then right again at the next traffic light. Near the corner is **Chomei-ji** 長命寺⑧ , which has a prosperous kindergarten attached. The temple is associated with the goddess Benten. In India she is worshiped as Sarasvati, the goddess of water, but in Japan she presides over music and eloquence and is therefore depicted holding a musical instrument in one of her hands. Although this temple has a history which dates back to the mid-sixteenth century, the present building is an uninteresting structure made almost entirely from concrete.

Next to this temple is **Kofuku-ji** 弘福寺⑨ , with its remark-able Chinese-style architecture. This temple is associated with Hotei, a sixth-century Chinese Zen priest, who is now consid-ered the god of popularity. He is usually depicted as a loosely clad, potbellied man. The shrine sells very pretty *ema* (wooden tablets) with pictures of the year's Chinese zodiacal animal. Especially fragrant cedar wood from Nikko is used, and the pictures are cleverly handpainted. Just as you approach the gate to leave, notice two ancient-looking stone statues of an old man and woman in an alcove to the left. With archaic smiles, they are supposed to be efficacious against coughing and have attracted worshipers since the mid-seventeenth century.

Leaving Kofuku-ji, turn right to enjoy a brief stroll through the heart of the famous Mukojima *hanamachi* (pleasure district) with many assignation houses and fine restaurants. Across the street from Kofukuji, a dark five-story building is a classically decorated restaurant with split bamboo screens and a stone lantern. Next to the temple is another special restaurant sur-rounded by boldly designed white walls. Past the traffic light, a relatively large gray building on the right is the *kemban,* an of-fice for making arrangements for geisha parties. A row of pa-per lanterns seen through second-story windows suggests a large room for music and dance lessons. The design of the two buildings beyond it also indicates their business in this trade. (These buildings might be observed better from the other side of the street.) Taking the next right, you will find a good sushi restaurant, **Murasaki-zushi** むらさき寿司 ⑩, which serves delicious sushi at reasonable prices. *(Open 12:00 to 0:30. Closed on Tuesdays.)*

Turn right at the next two corners to come back to the traffic light. Cross the intersection and continue straight until the third small crossing with a small shop marked by a blue-and-white banner in front. It specializes in *tabi*. Turn left at the shop and walk straight until you come to an irregular four-road crossing where you continue straight on (don't turn left). Past a school on the right, take the second small road to the right. This neighborhood escaped the destruction of air raids during World War II, and rows of old wooden homes and workshops remain as evidence of traditional lifestyles. An excellent craftsman, Nishiyama-san, lives here with his family, making beautiful *oshie hagoita* (Kabuki figures fixed on boards). The artist has opened part of his workshop for public viewing as the **Hagoita Shiryokan** 羽子板資料館 ⑪. It is located beyond a small liquor store at a small crossroads straight ahead. Take the narrow road between it and a tofu shop and look for the third building on the left.

Born in Asakusa and dedicated to his job for more than fifty years, Nishiyama-san makes irresistibly beautiful Kabuki figures using silk cloth, scissors, glue, and an old-fashioned hand iron. He is an enthusiastic Kabuki fan who can visualize almost any Kabuki character. Portraits of Kabuki actors in their successful roles are drawn on cardboard, which is cut into sections. The small pieces of paper are thinly padded with cotton and covered with carefully chosen fabrics. The padded parts are glued on the wooden board with the head slightly raised for enhanced dramatic effect. Over three-hundred steps are involved before the completion of one figure, from designing the sketch to selecting materials, including the most difficult part of the job, the face. His son, Kazuhiro, has joined him in his work, determined to inherit his father's skills and spirit. Even with these two specialists working from early morning till late at night, only a few hundred figures are available for sale each year. *(The Hagoita Shiryokan is open on Thursday, Friday, and Saturday, 10:00–17:00. For information, call 3623-1305.)*

Backtrack to the main road and turn right. The road soon meets a busy highway where you turn right and soon, past a brown building, bear right to take a smaller road which runs parallel to the highway.

At the end of the road, you come to a crossing with a shopping street. Turn left to the traffic light on the highway. At this corner is a small shrine surrounded by gingko trees and red banners. However, first turn left to visit a small shop called **Kibikoya** 吉備子屋 ⑫, selling simple dumplings made of millet. The small, skewered dumplings sprinkled with powdered roast soy beans used to be a favorite snack of Shitamachi children. A man who had grown up in this area learned the recipe from an old peddler and started this hutlike shop in the mid-1980s. In spite of the initial worries of local people and the shopkeeper himself, the shop has survived and serves as a good stopover for visitors on the lucky gods tour. You, too, might enjoy a bite of the inexpensive, healthy *kibi dango,* as they are sold nowhere else.

Now, cross over to the shrine; you will find the small space cluttered with half-eroded stone monuments and simple roofed structures. Often, people are seen washing some of the statues with water as they pray to them. The center of the worship is Jizo, housed under a roof on the left-hand side. The statue, vaguely discernible beyond a latticed door, was found in the early nineteenth century buried in mud on the bank of the Sumida River. Every month, on the 4, 14, and 24, a fair is held.

Behind the tiny sanctum, a small road forks out to the left, leading to the next destination. At the end of the road, which formerly was a cherry-bordered riverside walk, stands the gray stone torii of **Shirahige-jinja** 白髭神社 ⑬, a shrine originally founded in the middle of the tenth century. The name of the shrine, which means "white-bearded god," explains its affiliation with Jurojin, the god of longevity, usually depicted as

an old saint with a long gray goatee. The shrine had a beautifully weathered wooden main building, but it was burnt down
by arsonists in March 1990. Terrorists set fire to several old
shrines in protest against an ancient theocratic ritual held during Prince Akihito's enthronement ceremonies. In an extensive
fund-raising campaign, donations from all over the country
were received to cover the cost of reconstruction. The new
building will be of concrete to meet stringent fire regulations,
but will be in the same design as before. *(The annual festival is
held on the first weekend of June.)*

Leaving the shrine by its front gate, turn left and walk
straight along the road which curves slightly to the right. Soon,
the thickly wooded **Hyakkaen** 百花園 ⑭ can be seen on the
left. Before going in, turn right for a quick look at a unique rainwater recycling station called a *rojison* 路地尊 ⑮ . A hand
pump has been installed to draw water from an underground
tank which stocks rainwater gathered from the roofs of nearby
houses. The water is for emergency relief in case an earthquake
or some other disaster cuts off the water supply. This idea resulted from the ecological activities of local residents, and there
are several other similar *rojison* in this area.

Now, enter Hyakkaen, literally, "garden of one hundred
flowers." Though it is neither a shrine nor a temple, this place is
the residence of the sixth god, Fukurokuju, who is the Chinese
god of wealth and longevity. Its graceful entrance is to your
left, where you pay a small admission. Hyakkaen was laid out
by Sahara Kikuu, a retired antiques dealer who lived in the
early nineteenth century. As the property of a commoner, this
garden features a soft, spontaneous style, liberated from the
fastidious formalities of famous daimyo gardens built in the
Edo period. The difference in style can easily be seen when you
compare Hyakkaen with Yasuda Garden, also built in the Edo
period on the same side of the bank of the Sumida River.

When Sahara purchased this land for his retirement, he
asked his friends, most of whom were poets and writers, to
donate one plum tree each, and quickly collected over 360

trees. He and his friends often got together to view the plum blossoms or to enjoy other sophisticated pleasures which this once rustic setting afforded. Some of them, such as moon viewing and listening to chirping insects, continue (in August and September, respectively). Gradually, other plants associated with classical literature were added to the garden, as well as stones engraved with poems by Sahara and his friends.

Leaving the garden, turn left and left again around the corner of the small playground to walk straight ahead, crossing the main road. At the traffic light, turn left to come to Higashi Mukojima Station. Buy the least expensive ticket and take a train to Kanegafuchi, the next stop. Coming out of Kanegafuchi Station, turn right along the main road and at the first traffic light turn right again and take the road with railings along its right side. Keep straight until you come to a fork, where you should bear left and then take the next right. A beige Tobu Line train can sometimes be seen at the end of this road. Quite close to the tracks is **Tamon-ji** 多聞寺 ⑯ , with a charming thatched gate.

Tamon-ji's gate was built in 1718, and is one of the oldest structures in Tokyo. The temple is dedicated to Bishamon, clad in armor and holding a pike in his hand. According to a temple legend, the land used for the temple precinct used to be the abode of a certain badger. The animal was so incensed by the construction of the temple on its home that it caused all kinds of trouble in the neighborhood. One night the priest heard something heavy fall down in the main hall of the temple, and when he went to investigate, he found the dead body of the badger in front of the altar. Taking pity on the animal, the priest buried him in the temple precinct, and prayed for his future happiness. As I was thinking about this story, I glanced up at the roof and saw a cheeky badger face staring down at me!

Leaving the temple, turn right and retrace your steps to the station. The Asakusa-bound trains leave from the platform on the other side of the railway crossing where you buy tickets to the end of the line. For a break before returning home, try **Silvia** シルビア ⑰, a coffee shop and restaurant, situated on the second floor of a large pachinko parlor, on the right before the railway crossing. It is the only coffee shop in this old-fashioned area.

If you are not too tired, you might be interested in a stopover at a craft shop five minutes from Hikifune Station, two stops from Kanegafuchi. At Hikifune, turn right after handing in your ticket and then right again to walk along the exterior wall of the station. Turn left when you come to a small playground with swings and walk straight to a traffic light. Cross the street and, still keeping straight, take the next small street to the left. Turn right at the next crossing, between a grocery store and a liquor shop, and take the next alley to the left. The third building on the left is **Bokusenan** 墨泉庵 ⑱, which sells and displays traditional handmade crafts, many made by artisans living in Sumida Ward.

The owner of the shop is Shinsen Iura, an Edo-style *yūzen* silk dyer. Sympathetic to the struggle of his fellow craftsmen to preserve their skills, he conceived the idea of a place for the permanent display of handmade arts. Upstairs, arrangements can be made for groups to take a quick lesson in *yūzen* dying. *(For information, call 3614-3681. Open 11:00–18:00 throughout the year.)*

Tanuki soba o tabeta koto ga arimasuka?
(Have you had *tanuki* [badger] noodles?)

APPENDIXES

Events Calendar

January 1   The year's first visit to a temple or shrine. Senso-ji (p. 21) is one of the places in Tokyo which attracts large crowds of people, but any other major shrine or temple would also be fun to visit.

January 1–5, or 7, *shichifukujin* (p. 171) in areas such as Mukojima, Yanaka, Fukagawa, or Ningyocho.

January 7   Daikon Matsuri at Matsuchiyama Shoden (p. 34), 11:30–14:30.

January 8   Dondo, at Torigoe-jinja (p. 152), 13:00.

February 3 or 4   Setsubun (the last calendar day of winter). Bean throwing at major temples and shrines.

February 8   Hari Kuyo (used needles service) at Awashima-jinja, and Senso-ji.

February 15–March 15   Plum Blossom Festival at Yushima Tenjin.

February 10–early March   Sale of dolls for Doll Festival on March 3, in the Asakusa-bashi area (pp. 153–155).

March 18   Jigen-e, a festival celebrating Kannon as the Asakusa deity, at Senso-ji; includes a golden dragon dance.

April 8   Hana Matsuri, a festival to celebrate the birth of Lord Buddha, at Senso-ji, Tsukiji Hongan-ji, and other temples.

April 14–May 5   Tsutsuji Matsuri at Nezu-jinja (p. 113).

April 15   Daidai Kagura at Shinagawa-jinja (p. 137), performed by costumed dancers wearing old masks.

April 17   Annual Festival at Toshogu (p. 87).

May 5   Annual Festival at Suitengu (p. 57–58).

May 11, or the Sunday closest to this date—Annual Festival at Shitaya-jinja near the Ginza Line Inaricho Station.

May 14, or the weekend closest to this date—Kanda Myojin festival (pp. 73–75); full-scale every two years.

May, the third weekend
Sanja Matsuri, the festival
of Asakusa-jinja (pp. 24–
25).

May 25, or the Sunday closest
to this date—Annual
festival of Yushima Tenjin
(pp. 76–77).

May 28   Festival of Koami-
jinja (p. 65).

June 7, or the weekend closest
to this date—Kappa
Matsuri at Ebara-jinja (p.
137), and Tenno-sai at
Shinagawa-jinja.

June 7, or the weekend closest
to this date—festival of
Shirahige-jinja (pp. 179–
180).

June 7, or the Sunday closest
to this date —festival of
Torigoe-jinja (p. 152).

June 8, or Sunday closest to
this date—Annual festival
at Namiyoke-jinja (p. 127).

July 6–8   Asagao Ichi (morn-
ing glory fair) at Iriya Kishi
Mojin near the Hibiya Line
Iriya Station.

July 9–10   Shiman Rokusen-
Nichi (forty-six thousand
days), at Senso-ji. A visit to
the temple on one of these
two days is supposed to be
equal to forty-six thousand
visits, with all the benefits
afforded to lucky visitors.
Stalls fill the compound to
sell potted *hozuki* (lantern
plants) and *furin* (wind
chimes).

July 13–15   Bon-odori at
Tsukudajima (pp. 124–
125).

Mid-July to mid-August
Summer festival at Shi-
nobazu Pond (p. 92).

July, last Saturday   Fireworks
on the Sumida River (p.
147).

August 6, or the weekend
closest to this date—
Annual festival at Sumiyoshi-jinja (p. 123); full-scale
festival every two years.

August 15   Bon sutra service
at Senso-ji at 6:30 P.M.,
followed by lantern
floating on the Sumida
River.

August 15, or the weekend
closest to this date—
Tomioka Hachiman
festival (pp. 160–161); full-
scale festival every three
years.

August 15–17 Fukagawa
Shimmeigu (p. 167)
summer festival.

September 20–21 Nezu-jinja
festival; Kagura performed
on 21st.

September 25 Doll service at
Kiyomizu Kannon (p. 86).

October 14–15 Chrysanthemum Festival at Daien-ji

(p. 106); dance performance in the evening.

October 18 Chrysanthemum Festival at Senso-ji; each worshiper carries a chrysanthemum to the temple and exchanges it for other chrysanthemums offered to the Kannon by the temple. The golden dragon dance is performed.

Mid–October to mid– November Chrysanthemum flower contest and exhibition at Senso-ji.

November 3 White Crane Dance at Senso-ji. Girls in white bird costumes perform a slow-tempo dance based on a legend. Also, Tokyo Jidai Matsuri features a grand pageant of historic characters in costumes, 13:30–15:30.

November 15, or the Sunday before—Shichi-Go-San, or Seven-Five-Three Festival at Asakusa-jinja (pp. 24–25), Tomioka Hachiman (pp. 160–161), and other major shrines. Five-year-old boys, seven- and three-year-old girls, all dressed up, visit a shrine with their parents to celebrate the

child's healthy growth. They return from the shrine carrying long paper bags containing stick candy.

November, on days of the bird Lucky Rake Fair at Otori-jinja (pp. 31–32), Tomioka Hachiman, Ebara-jinja, and other shrines related to this fair.

December 14 The Forty-Seven Ronin Festival at both Sengaku-ji (pp. 31–32) and the site of Lord Kira's house (p. 146).

December 17-19 Battledore Fair at Senso-ji.

Mid–December to December 27 or 28 The Year-end Fair at Senso-ji. Various materials used in the New Year's decoration of homes and shops are sold.

December 28 The year's last *ennichi* at Fukagawa Fudo (pp. 159–160).

December 31 The New Year's Eve bell ringing at major temples. Most temples all over the country ring their bells 108 times at midnight to drive out the 108 sins which are believed to prevent people from attaining salvation.

Index